Using Technology to Improve Reading and Learning

Authors

Colin Harrison, Ph.D.

Bernadette Dwyer, Ph.D.

Jill Castek, Ph.D.

Foreword

Donald J. Leu, Ph.D.

Elizabeth Calhoon, M.S.

SHELL EDUCATION

Publishing Credits

Robin Erickson, *Production Director*; Lee Aucoin, *Creative Director*;
Timothy J. Bradley, *Illustration Manager*; Sara Johnson, M.S.Ed., *Editorial Director*;
Maribel Rendón, M.A.Ed., *Editor*; Sara Sciuto, *Assistant Editor*;
Grace Alba Le, *Designer*; Corinne Burton, M.A.Ed., *Publisher*

Standards

© Copyright 2010. National Governors Association Center for Best Practices and Council of Chief State School Officers. All rights reserved.

Shell Education

5301 Oceanus Drive
Huntington Beach, CA 92649-1030
http://www.shelleducation.com
ISBN 978-1-4258-1314-7
© 2014 Shell Educational Publishing, Inc.

Table of Contents

FOREWORDS

We have entered a highly globalized world of reading and learning, and *Using Technology to Improve Reading and Learning* leads the way. This is the first book devoted to classroom instruction, in both traditional and cutting-edge literacies, that has been written in collaboration by leading scholars from three different nations—Dr. Colin Harrison from England, Dr. Bernadette Dwyer from Ireland, and Dr. Jill Castek from the United States. Most importantly, each of these authors is also a profoundly talented teacher with many years of experience. They speak with a knowledgeable teacher's voice from the classroom.

The Internet and other technologies are a profoundly shifting force, regularly altering many elements of society. These technologies are also transforming the nature of reading and learning as we shift from page to screen, where new tools continuously appear, calling for new skills and strategies in reading, writing, and communication. Moreover, the new literacies now required to read in our world are not just new today, but as the latest tools for reading, learning, and communicating are introduced, they each necessitate the acquisition of new skills, strategies, dispositions, and social practices. How we adapt in this changing world of reading and learning will define how well our students are prepared for their future.

Collaborations like the one in this book enable us to succeed in our classrooms during challenging times. Colin, Bernadette, and Jill have provided us with a highly readable and, most importantly, teachable volume to guide us into this modern world of classroom literacy and learning. We are able to obtain the very best instructional ideas from changing classroom contexts in three different nations, not just one. In addition, these ideas are connected to an important learning framework, the Common Core State Standards that are currently emerging in the U.S.

You and your students will be transformed and energized by the ideas in this book; I was. The authors have shown us a path that will enable our students to become the highly literate and knowledgeable citizens the world now demands.

Donald J. Leu, Ph.D.
The John and Maria Neag Endowed Chair in Literacy and Technology
University of Connecticut

It is without a doubt that teachers are no longer the holders of all information; rather, we are the master curators, facilitators of learning, and champions of curiosity. This shift in the role of the teacher is recent, fast-paced, and incredibly scary. But like all change, it is also constant, inspiring, and the greatest challenge our educational system has ever faced.

There are few books that actually provide practical, pragmatic advice and support for educators who are looking for guidance on how to shift their own learning (and teaching) to become lead learners, and the teachers we all know we can be. The real effectiveness of *Using Technology to Improve Reading and Learning* lies in its clarity and brief dives into the essence of effective learning technologies' instructional practices. For example, cell phones have been controversial in an educational setting, but they are hugely popular with many teachers. For those of you who haven't made up your minds about them yet, this book provides a succinct, clear argument for their use in the classroom, backed up with common-sense rationale.

In my work as an instructional technology lead learner/facilitator/support-system/shoulder-to-cry-on/cheerleader, I've had the opportunity to work with educators worldwide who have opinions of their own technical expertise that are as wide as the Amazon River. Many people assess their tech-pertise based on others' perception. When we are just beginning to explore how to really leverage technology, we are limited by our geography, by our past experiences with technology, and by our colleagues' perception of us. The challenge then becomes to find a way to get a real, accurate assessment of your skills so that, and here's the important part, *you know where you need to grow.* If you don't know where to grow, you are guaranteed to never get there. I prefer to look at my own growth through my interest level *and* my skill level. When it comes to technology, I'd encourage you to start assessing each chapter in this book with that lens and open up to the possibility that both interest and skill are things you can change, and increase, with enough perseverance. I'd also highly encourage you to use the "Questions for Reflections" to reflect on the ideas in this book, as it helped me re-center my thinking and instructional practices.

No matter where you think your interest and skill levels are, have fun with this book. It's a fantastic resource to come back to over and over again. Read some of the books in the References Cited—some are central to the thinking of the greatest educators' minds today. Most of all, learn…learn a lot. Because it is all going to be okay, and this is a fun book!

Elizabeth Calhoon, M.S.
Google™ Certified Teacher
Past ISTE Innovative Technologies Professional Development Chair

ACKNOWLEDGMENTS

The authors wish to thank the many colleagues, students, teachers and principals with whom we have worked in the USA, Ireland, and the UK in order to develop and evaluate the resources in this book. Without their cooperation, creativity, and cheerful assistance, we would have had no worthwhile story to tell.

To our friends at Shell Education, our thanks for your inspiring creativity, your enthusiasm for our work, and your encouragement to get the job done.

Finally, to our families and loved ones, thank you for your support; we couldn't have done this without you.

CHAPTER 1

Using Technology to Make the Teaching of Literacy More Exciting

In this chapter, you will learn:

- how this book can help you become a more confident and a more effective teacher;

- why the authors are confident that this book will be helpful for you; and

- three ways in which you might use this book.

After reading this chapter, you will understand:

- that the authors of this book do not believe technology will solve every problem; and

- that developing students' critical Internet literacy is one of a teacher's most important jobs.

Why You Need This Book

The aim of this book is to help teachers improve their students' reading, writing, and communication skills, and particularly to help teachers become more confident in using technology to make the teaching of literacy more exciting, more engaging, and more effective.

Do you want to develop the following in your students?

- literacy
- vocabulary
- comprehension
- fluency
- critical thinking
- skills in synthesizing
- creativity
- engagement
- autonomy
- planning skills
- teamwork skills
- Internet criticality
- collaborative learning

Do you feel you need to know more about how technology can help you to achieve these goals? If the answers to both these questions are "yes," then this book is for you.

Computers have been in classrooms since the 1980s, but in many schools, the usage of technology to enhance learning and empower learners has hardly changed since those early days. Yet in other schools—in economically disadvantaged districts as well as rich districts—teachers and students are using computers and other devices in every lesson, and students' learning and their achievement have been transformed. How can it be that while there is broad agreement about how to teach reading, there are massive differences between how teachers in different schools use technology? National and state policies drive the reading curriculum, and therefore the teaching of literacy is delivered using materials and approaches that are broadly similar. This, however, does not apply to teachers' use of technology.

We know from research that different teachers have completely different professional experiences when it comes to professional development and support in using new technologies. We also know from research, from over 30 years ago, that it's no good to simply present teachers with computers, tablets, electronic whiteboards, or video cameras. If teachers are not given support and professional development, they will not use them.

The picture is changing rapidly and in two very significant ways. First, many teachers who say "I'm not really a technology person" are in fact increasingly competent with technology: they own and use a computer every day, they use other devices such as a phone and digital camera, and they already use technology in their teaching, at least some of the time. Second, teachers' access to support has changed radically. Research into teachers' use of computers in the 1990s showed that those who had access to informal networks of support (for example, a close colleague who could show them what to do, or a teaching partner or neighbor who was knowledgeable) learned more and became more confident than those who only received professional development from experts in a more formal school setting (Harrison et al. 1998). However, teachers today have access to many more sources of ideas, guidance, and informal learning. To begin with, their students—collectively, at least—often know more than their teachers about how to use the Internet, how to share files, and how to make and edit multimedia. The other key resource for informal and just-in-time learning is the Internet itself. The 25 billion pages of the Internet contain tens of thousands of lesson ideas and thousands of videos for teachers. At the time of this writing, a Google™ search for the verbatim phrase *videos for teachers* offered nearly a million links, some of which were to sites that offered over 3,000 videos.

This book will help you learn more about what resources are available out there to support your teaching. However, resources alone are not enough. Teaching is a social as well as a cognitive activity, and, as a teacher, you need to know how to organize your students and their learning in order to make the best use of technology. Every teaching idea in this book has been used, and used successfully, in day-to-day school contexts and mostly in schools in economically challenged areas. The authors are classroom teachers who became college professors, but each of them has continued to spend part of their year in classrooms, teaching and evaluating new software and hardware, and road-testing new ideas. They know how to engage those students who are the most challenging to teach: the weaker readers, those who lack the confidence or social skills to work collaboratively, those whose language skills are only emerging, and those whose learning needs a good deal of scaffolding.

Nearly every teacher these days can use PowerPoint® in his or her instruction, and that's a good thing. A digital presentation requires planning, organization, and the ability to connect hardware and software to a data projector. A good presentation can hold the attention of a class (at least for a while!) and may be the focus for a brilliant expository lesson. But some teachers have used the phrase *Death by PowerPoint* to describe lessons in which the slide show presentation is used in no more creative a manner than a chalkboard was a hundred years ago—to present a sequence of textbook pages for copying as the teacher simply reads the text aloud. This can leave the students bored and disconnected from any engagement with the material. It is this approach that Tom Fishburne tried to capture in the cartoon found in Figure 1.1. We know we can do better!

Figure 1.1 We Know We Can Do Better!

Printed with Permission from Marketoonist LLC

Finally, but very importantly, this book is necessary because the skills that students need to acquire are new, and teachers need to learn what these new skills are and how to develop them in their students. Twenty years ago, every school textbook went through a dozen stages of editing and adoption before it came into the classroom, and textbooks would be replaced in a regular cycle by newer, more authoritative editions. Today, schools in the United States and Europe are buying fewer textbooks, and, at the same time, students are relying more on Internet sources. This creates a serious problem because, while textbooks have the authority of established authors and publishers behind them, anyone can publish on the Internet. In this brave new postmodern world, students, and especially younger learners, can be at serious risk. They don't know how easy it is for any group to set up a site that willfully mimics a legitimate site, and then subverts it. They don't know how to evaluate and adjudicate between Web sources, and they don't know how to summarize or transform the information they locate in order to make good use of it. The authors of this book have been dealing with this challenge head-on in classrooms on both sides of the Atlantic, and if you adopt the teaching approaches that are shared in the pages that follow, you will not only find some great lesson ideas, you will take a major step forward in developing critical Internet literacy in your classroom.

Why the Authors Are Able to Help You

There are three reasons why you should feel confident this book will help you to become an even better teacher.

1. **We are all teachers.** We are teachers who love creating those joyful moments in classrooms when the students not only learn, but become so engrossed in their learning that they sigh with disappointment when it's time for the lesson to end and beg you to let them carry on working, even though it's lunch time or time to go home.

2. **We are all experienced in the professional development of teachers.** We know that it's not helpful to just show a video of a brilliant teacher giving a virtuoso performance in the classroom and invite you to copy him or her because this can simply make a less experienced teacher feel that there is an unbridgeable gulf between him or her and a more expert colleague. What we know as experienced professional developers is that the best way to help teachers is to instill confidence about what they already know, and then to help them move forward in small steps, supported not only by lesson plans and good ideas, but by encouraging voices from real classrooms that make them feel they're not making the journey alone.

3. **We are researchers who have been working in the United States, in Ireland, and in the United Kingdom in a wide range of schools,** with some of the most talented, knowledgeable, and inspirational experts in new technology on the planet. This has connected us to some wonderful teachers and some inspirational teaching.

Colin Harrison began as a high school English teacher, and he has been teaching using computers in elementary and high school classrooms since 1980. Figure 1.2 shows him with a class of 12-year-olds in 1984. The students had been writing adventure stories based on Pac-Man™, a very simple computer game in which ghosts chase an animated chomping mouth around a maze. From this educationally questionable start, he went on to lead over 40 research projects evaluating the use of computers in schools. He has been involved in a number of transatlantic studies of computer use and pan-European studies of technology in schools. He is a former president of the UK Reading Association, he chaired the Technology and Literacy Committee of the International Reading Association from 2001–2004, and he has directed six national evaluations of technology and teacher development for the UK government. But his work has not only been at policy level. Between 1980 and 2010, there were only five years in which he did not teach at least once a week in a local school, wherever possible bringing together technology and literacy development.

Figure 1.2 Colin Harrison Working with the BBC Model B Computer, Helping Students Publish their Pac-Man Adventure Stories in 1984

Printed with permission from Fairham Community School

Bernadette Dwyer began as a primary school teacher, where she taught at all grade levels before becoming especially interested in meeting the needs of those students who need extra support for learning. She currently works in teacher education in Dublin, where she has taken a special interest in reading development and online reading comprehension, two themes to which she gave particular prominence during her recent time as president of the Reading Association of Ireland. Her doctoral study focused on the use of the Internet in an inquiry-based elementary school classroom in one of the most economically disadvantaged areas of Dublin, and what she learned from the two years in which she worked in that school has contributed a great deal to the chapters in this book. Bernadette is a member of the Board of Directors of the International Reading Association (2013–2016).

Jill Castek began her career as a teacher in high school special education classes for students who struggled with basic literacy. After earning a K–12 reading specialist credential and a masters degree, she specialized in supporting the literacy development of students at the elementary level, many of whom were English language learners. Jill's interest in computers for learning led her to join one of the most respected literacy and technology research groups in the world—the New Literacies Research Team at the University of Connecticut—where she completed her doctoral study on the development of students' comprehension during online learning. She then worked on the influential Seeds of Science/Roots of Reading project, a cross-curricular initiative that brings together the teaching of science, literacy, and technology in order to give students skills that are not only valuable in elementary and middle grades but are also going to be valuable to them in high school, college, and beyond.

Schools change slowly, but the world doesn't wait for schools to change. The world is becoming more interconnected every day. These thoughts are scary, but we need to remember that we are teaching people who are going to be alive 75 years from now, and that the pace of change will never be slower than it is now. The world will change in ways we can only begin to imagine, but two things we can be reasonably sure of—it will be interconnected in richer and even more complex ways, and it will still need education systems that use technology to promote not only communication but also equity, freedom of thought, and responsible knowledge. Our aim as authors is not just to help you become an even better teacher but also to help you become a teacher who is inspired rather than threatened by new technologies and who is determined to help students become successful users of technologies not yet invented in an ever more interconnected world.

How This Book Is Organized

Our goal as authors is not to persuade you to use technology. We are not evangelists for hardware, for software, or for the Internet. In fact, each of us believes strongly that the most important person in the classroom is the teacher, not the computer, and that there are many occasions when it may well be downright wrong to use the computer. We believe in the joy of holding a book, in sharing a book, and in reading a poem aloud as well as in the delight of helping a printed book capture the hearts and minds of students.

But there are times, and perhaps an increasing number of times, when it is appropriate to use a computer, and our goals are therefore twofold:

- To help you set up learning opportunities in ways that make technology your ally rather than your rival, and

- To help you to be a more confident and knowledgeable user of technology, as a result of which your students will become confident and more highly motivated readers, more skilled navigators, and more critical users of information.

In order to help you, we have written this book with an emphasis on one central set of resources: strategies for the classroom. We make the assumption that you already have a rich repertoire of professional skills, and that you also understand that you need to augment that repertoire because many aspects of reading are changed by new technologies.

The strategies have been divided into categories by chapter:

- Strategies for Capitalizing on What Students Already Know (Chapter 2)

- Strategies for Using Digital Tools to Support Literacy Development (Chapter 3)

- Strategies for Using eReaders and Digital Books to Expand the Reading Experience (Chapter 4)

- Strategies for Teaching the Information-Seeking Cycle: The Process of Searching for Information on the Internet (Chapter 5)

- Strategies for Teaching the Information-Seeking Cycle: The Product Stage of Searching for Information on the Internet (Chapter 6)

- Strategies for Encouraging Peer Collaboration and Cooperative Learning (Chapter 7)

- Strategies for Building Communities of Writers (Chapter 8)

- Strategies for Building Teachers' Capacity to Make the Most of New Technologies (Chapter 9)

Most teachers believe that a student can only learn if the new material is at their Zone of Proximal Development (ZPD)—the zone where their prior knowledge can provide secure scaffolding for new learning (Vygotsky 1978). And, of course, the same applies to teachers. As authors, our hope is that you feel that while this list of strategies seems challenging and valuable, you also feel that you have some useful scaffolding upon which to build this additional knowledge.

We have good news for any reader who feels that his or her background knowledge is woefully thin: you are not alone. Many, many teachers with whom we have worked on professional development have confessed to feeling a little inadequate around new technology. It is precisely for this reason that we begin in Chapter 2 with strategies that build upon not what you know, but what your students already know.

As many teachers have already discovered, students know a great deal about new technologies. Unlike some grown-ups, they generally do not try to make those who know less than they do feel inadequate. Students are often enthusiastic and generous-spirited teachers who are delighted to find that they have skills or knowledge that they can share. Chapter 2 introduces you to a variety of ways in which this knowledge can be shared in beneficial ways.

In the chapters that follow, the authors present dozens of strategies that link to skills that most teachers already possess as well as to the Common Core State Standards, which lay out clearly what students are expected to learn in U.S. classrooms. We encourage you to enhance your expertise and to try new approaches, but we will never ask you to abandon your own professional proficiency and knowledge. The strategies that we offer have all been extensively tested in a range of classrooms, in different countries, and with a variety of school populations, and they draw upon a deep research base. We try never to leave you feeling alone and isolated; instead, we try to share the voices of students and teachers to help sustain and support you, and we offer many links to the good practice of others, extending your professional contacts using a range of different networking opportunities.

Many of the strategies and the key arguments of the book are presented in the chapter text, but we have also tried to present some of our ideas in a variety of other ways to make them easier to locate and use. We've made use of different types of call-outs, each of which serves a different function. Each call-out is presented in its own distinctive format. We hope that you will find these really useful. Figure 1.3 explains the nature of each call-out.

Figure 1.3 Our Call-Outs and What Each Is Trying to Achieve

Call-Out	What This Call-Out Does
Voices from the Classroom	We believe that the authentic voices of students and teachers have a special place in making our book compelling and valuable for other teachers.
Classroom Connection	Lesson plans and ideas can be incredibly helpful, even more so when they capture the moment of teaching and learning.
Pause for Thought	Time for reflection is so precious, especially when a teacher is trying out new ideas and approaches.
Common Core to the Fore	All good teaching is anchored to goals that are part of a larger plan, and here, we can connect our reading and technology objectives with broader curriculum goals.

Connections to Common Core Standards: The Knowledge and Skills That Your Students Will Gain

The Common Core State Standards represent an attempt to bring some coherence and cohesion to U.S. educational efforts by both capturing the essence of the curriculum goals of individual states and aligning them with future college and workplace expectations. In this respect, the Standards have much in common with national curriculum goals in other English-speaking nations, most of which have adopted a similar approach and have tried to bring rigor and coherence to the curriculum while at the same time ensuring that there is an emphasis on higher-order thinking and the new skills needed in our developing societies.

The U.S. standards have been developed following an international benchmarking exercise, and our hope, therefore, is that by offering points of correlation to Common Core Standards, we shall be assisting not only U.S. teachers but also those from other countries to link their teaching to these important goals.

How to Use This Book

The chapters in this book form a logical sequence, but each is freestanding and may be used on its own as a support for your personal learning or for group professional development. We want to encourage you to try out many of the strategies that we propose, but where should you begin?

We suggest three possible starting points:

- **Starting point one is Chapter 2.** Perhaps the easiest place to begin is by finding out what your students already know. The Classroom Connection in Chapter 2 addresses the question *How can you make the best use of technology that your students possess, and the skills they have in using it?* Collecting this information could be an invaluable starting point for your students to begin sharing expertise with one another, but they will also be sharing it with you!

- **Starting point two would be for you to choose a chapter title that you feel resonates with some knowledge or a particular interest that you already have.** If you are already confident in developing comprehension, for example, you could begin with Chapter 6, *Strategies For Teaching the Information-Seeking Cycle: The Process of Searching for Information on the Internet.* If you already enjoy setting up peer collaboration and cooperative learning, you could begin with Chapter 7, *Strategies for Encouraging Peer Collaboration and Cooperative Learning.* Whichever chapter you choose, we are confident that the lesson ideas in these chapters are approachable, but that they will also take you into new areas of professional expertise.

- **Starting point three would be to begin with Chapter 9,** *Strategies for Building Teachers' Capacity to Make the Most of New Technologies.* One reason for doing this would be that the chapter offers advice on how to set up networks and new online professional communities. The chapter contains many examples of how to establish and sustain such communities. If you began here, you would be planning on sharing plans, ideas, and resources with other colleagues from the outset. If you follow the plans, you will be on your way to success.

As authors who are themselves continually seeking to expand our knowledge of how to make the best use of new technologies, we know that there will be unanticipated changes in hardware and software during the coming years. But the ideas that we share in this book will not rapidly go out of date. The new skills that your students need to develop and hone are not ones that will change, even if educational policy changes. The skills needed to develop reading and literacy will not change; the skills needed to be able to navigate, critique, and transform the billions of pages of information available through the Internet will not change; the need to develop literacy skills for life in the world after school will not change.

Our responsibilities as teachers are daunting. Some politicians may believe that the responsibilities of a teacher are to develop literacy and instill knowledge. How little such people understand about the real reasons why teachers work night and day. Teachers work ceaselessly because they are engaged in the most important "manufacturing job" of all—making knowledgeable people. As teachers work with parents on that daunting task, they know with certainty that literacy and knowledge alone are not enough and that five hours a day are not enough. Our students, the citizens and parents of tomorrow, will learn as much from the Internet as from their teachers; they will be creators of knowledge as well as consumers of knowledge, and their ability to use technology not only to communicate but to set up collaborative and equitable networks will be an essential life skill. As teachers we need to do all we can to help students develop the skills of literacy, understanding, criticality, and social responsibility that will enable them to use technology not simply to make their lives more interesting but also to make the world a better place. As authors who are also teachers, we sincerely hope that this book will make a contribution to supporting your professional development as you take on this vital work.

Questions for Reflection

1. Does the expression *Death by PowerPoint* sound familiar? Has your own use of PowerPoint® changed over the last couple of years? If so, in what ways has it changed?

2. How do you feel about students bringing their own devices into class? Some teachers are happy to encourage this. Are they naïve, or are they ahead of their time?

3. How do you perceive your own responsibilities in relation to teaching critical Internet literacy?

4. The authors all believe working with a colleague can make learning both more fun and more productive as you learn together from each other. Can you identify a colleague or a small group of colleagues with whom you might work in trying out some of the ideas in this book?

CHAPTER 2

Strategies for Capitalizing on What Students Already Know

In this chapter, you will learn:

- some of the ways in which the lives of students are being changed by new technologies;

- why we should not feel threatened by the fact that our students may know more than we do about how to use digital tools;

- that for many students, participating in online activities is teaching them valuable skills and making them smarter; and

- that the mobile phone may be a more powerful learning tool worldwide than a computer.

After reading this chapter, you will:

- understand two key principles of working with students who are ahead of you in using technology, that students can become co-workers, and that in using new technologies, you do not have to abandon traditional teaching approaches;

- know how to map and make use of your students' knowledge of new technologies;

- know how to set up a wiki that will engage and motivate students; and

- have encountered 14 ways of bringing Web 2.0 teaching into your classroom.

They'll Learn from Me, I'll Learn from Them

Geoff, a high school art teacher with 30 years of experience, comments on how his students have helped to make him a confident user of technology: "How has technology changed my teaching?" he asks. "Drastically. We teach one another now...the software normally has five or six different ways to bring about a solution. They'll find them all. They'll teach me new ways. I'll teach them the way that I know, and they'll come up with different solutions all the time. So it's absolutely fascinating. They'll learn from me, I'll learn from them."

The Bad News: Students Know More than We Do

To many teachers, the pace of technological change is frightening. It isn't slowing down. Computing performance (as measured by Moore's Law—see the graph in Figure 2.1) has roughly doubled every year since 1970, and the trend is set to continue for a few years. As nanotransistors begin to approach the size of atoms, this trend will slow down, but developments in memory, screen, and camera technologies have already brought us to a world we could hardly have imagined 50 years ago. The mobile phones that so many of our students bring to class (in most schools, they still tend to be hidden in bags and turned off *some* of the time) not only have access to the 25 billion pages of the Internet, but they can also process email, record video in high-definition, function as a GPS, hold dozens of books, and permit international videoconferencing. New applications offer online TV and newspaper content from all over the world and even instant language translation of text viewed through the video camera.

For teachers, this presents a real problem. In the past, dedicated educators have traditionally been two or three steps ahead of their students, and this has enabled them to go into class confident that they have new knowledge to impart. However, this model of education is changing. Schools are structurally conservative institutions and tend to be slow to react to external forces, but new technologies don't wait—their impact on our world is driven by powerful market dynamics, and these don't ask for the school board's permission to change the nature of education. Today, access to knowledge is not determined by who has a college degree but by who has the better technology. Often, it's students rather than the teacher who have the better technology.

Figure 2.1 Moore's Law: The Number of Transistors on a Computer Chip Has Roughly Doubled Every Two Years Since 1970

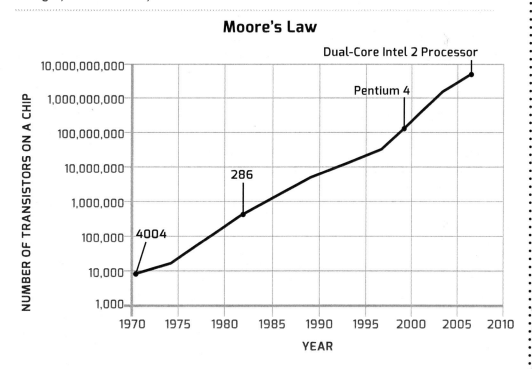

The Good News: What Your Students Know Is Valuable, and What We Know Is Different from What They Know

But there is good news, which we can express as two principles:

- **First Principle:** In the new world of technology in education, our students can become our co-workers, allies, and assistants rather than our competitors or adversaries.

- **Second Principle:** If our teaching approaches are the right ones, they work just as well, or even better, in a world that makes effective use of new technology.

Let's look, for example, at Geoff. We met him while working on a research project whose purpose was to report on how teachers in high-technology schools were using computers. Geoff told us that his whole approach to education had changed during the past five years, and what he had to say about this change illustrates both our principles. As his words demonstrate (see the *Voices from the Classroom* at the beginning of this chapter), technology has changed his teaching "drastically." His students have become his co-workers, and he's no longer intimidated by the fact that collectively they know more about the technology than he does. He has also completely changed how he teaches, and has opened up his teaching resources and even his lesson plans to his students. More of Geoff's story is shared below.

> *One lovely little instance was a [sixth-grade] girl who saw me on Wednesday and said "I hope you don't mind, I've been looking at your resources. I've done the next three pieces of homework that you've assigned, and I've also worked two or three pages ahead. Is that all right?"*

Five years ago, Geoff would never have dreamt of sharing his plans for a whole semester with his students, but now they can all see his planning online, and he's happy with the freedom this gives his students:

> *That is why it's there. That's fantastic. She printed the work off at home and brought it in in a file, which was just lovely.*

Throughout this book, we shall attempt to demonstrate both of these principles—working with our students and adapting our teaching to use technology more effectively—in a very practical series of ways, with lesson plans, case studies, and examples that make use of the latest research from all over the world.

In the Classroom Connection that follows, we suggest one way in which you might make a start on this journey simply by finding out what your students know, and what skills they possess that might be valuable to you and to one another. It's probably not a good idea to ask directly what technology students have at home—this might be divisive or intrusive. However, if you try to find out what skills they have, you will inevitably find out a good deal about the technologies to which they have access, and this could be an important step in your making better use of their knowledge.

The Classroom Connection suggests how you might conduct an informal audit of your students' knowledge and skills with technology. You can decide the best way to encourage your students to complete an *I can...* list, depending on your local circumstances and the age of the group. It's a good idea to get started by including some answers that everyone will be able to write down, whether it's *make a call on a mobile phone* or *save my work on the computer.*

Classroom Connection

Conducting an Audit of Your Students' Skills

How best can you make use of the technology that your students possess and the skills they have in using it?

You might ask students to write an *I can...* list of the skills they already have and then add more possible skills suggested by members of the class. This might be turned into a whole-class graph:

> *I can...* make a phone call
>
> *I can...* use a camera on a phone
>
> *I can...* play a game on a phone
>
> *I can...* do a search on Google™
>
> *I can...* view a video on YouTube™

> We can...

A chart of the skills possessed by the group as a whole could be an invaluable starting point for the students to begin sharing expertise with one another, as well as with their teacher!

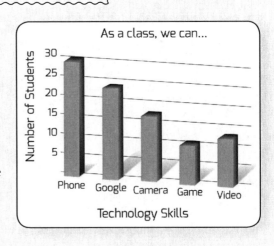

To ensure that you gain some information about your students' newly acquired skills (which may include some that you don't possess as of yet), ask them to think of five skills that they possess that they didn't have a year ago. It is also useful to get students to share their ideas, both to remind others of skills they might have forgotten that they have, but also to alert you to how much collective knowledge there is in the group.

 # Common Core to the Fore

Preparing Students to Meet the Common Core

Arguably, the most influential reform in the last five years has been the movement toward a set of Common Core State Standards (CCSS). The CCSS map out national benchmarks that outline the expected knowledge and skills students need to acquire to be college- and career-ready at the end of their K–12 education. The CCSS target the application of knowledge through higher-order cognitive skills such as analysis, synthesis, and evaluation. This movement toward a national set of standards has transformed curriculum development efforts and assessment approaches, so they are aligned in a more targeted way toward these benchmarks. Knowing what students know and can do, and building on the collective knowledge they possess, goes a long way in helping you proactively plan to address these standards. Instructional approaches that emphasize literacy across the curriculum and use of digital technologies for reading, writing, and communication are important places to start. Integrating process skills such as collaboration, listening, and speaking are also central to meeting the CCSS.

A central theme of this chapter is that students bring to school a great deal of knowledge that can be valuable for them and valuable to you, as their teacher. In the following sections of the chapter, we look at what research tells us about the types of knowledge that they have and how it can be applied in the classroom.

What Are Kids Learning from Games, and How Can This Be Useful to Their Teachers?

Computer games excite mixed emotions among teachers and parents. We may not like the value system of a war game, or of a game that glorifies violent crime. We may not like the fact that some students, and particularly boys, spend many hours a week playing computer games. But are students damaged by games, or do they learn anything useful from them? Research has consistently shown that video games do not make students more violent (Ferguson et al. 2012). Teachers worry because games can be addictive, and they seem to substitute virtual reality for the real world of relationships. The number of games sold is mind-boggling. According to Wikipedia (2014), over 40 million copies of *Super Mario Brothers*™, and over 150 million units of *The Sims*™ have been sold worldwide. Perhaps it is reassuring that the biggest-selling games are not first-person shoot 'em up blood-baths but games involving problem solving and complex multi-variable scenario development in a world of human avatars.

James Gee (a cognitive scientist) is interested in games focused on learning. He asks the question *What is it about video games that motivate students to want to play them?* His answers are important ones for us to consider. What Gee noticed was that many students devoted a great deal of their time (and money) to playing long, complex, and challenging video games for a reason, and this was that they were learning—and they were enjoying learning. Far from seeing game players as sociopathic zombies, he argued that game players were engaging in meaningful new experiences, and these experiences had the potential to make people smarter and more thoughtful. Gee developed his argument in detail (Gee 2003, 2005, 2008), and some of his key findings were:

- In a good video game (and Gee cited many that he felt were good), the players **are active and not passive learners**; they co-create the world in which they play, and their decisions and actions matter.

- In a good video game, **players make decisions about what and how they will learn**; they can play the game in entirely different scenarios and at the level they choose to give them the right balance of challenge and achievement.

- Good games **offer the player an opportunity to determine his or her own identity**, either by adopting a persona and entering into a new role, or by offering an identity template that can be manipulated and augmented by the player.

- Good games **offer players a chance to manipulate their environment** in ways that permit both more enjoyment and deeper learning, and they do so by discovering parts of the deeper rule set that underpins the logic of the game world.

- Good games **take place in a problem space that feels free** but is in reality a highly structured environment in which the problems are "pleasantly frustrating."

- Good games **alternate between practice** (gaining mastery) **and challenge** (developing new skills).

- Good games **introduce new information "just in time"** rather than all at the beginning, and complex verbal information is best delivered "on demand."

- Good games **offer "fish tanks"**—small ecosystems in which a learner can work in a scaled-down world before encountering the complexity of the full game, or **"sandboxes"**—playful environments in which the risks are fewer and consequences are less dramatic.

- People learn best when they **understand how what they are learning fits into the bigger picture**.

The implications of Gee's argument are clear. As teachers, we would do well to ask ourselves how we can integrate some of these principles into our own teaching. He suggests that the brilliant designers who wove these principles into their games should be our teachers. How might we do this? If we answer the questions below, we can start to address how we might learn from our students how to increase both their learning and their motivation:

- How can we make students active rather than passive learners?
  How can we develop agents and producers, rather than followers and consumers?

- How can we offer students a wider choice of learning pathways, through which they can take different routes?

- How can we offer learners an identity space within which they can make choices, project fantasies, and pursue their chosen goals?

- How can our learners manipulate the learning environment to make it a closer fit for their preferred ways of learning, and then offer them deep learning experiences within that environment?

- How can we offer information and learning opportunities in different modalities and on a "just in time" basis?

- How can we offer learners exciting but less risky environments for learning in which progress is certain but failure isn't damaging, humiliating, or costly?

- How can we offer learning opportunities that are authentic, worthwhile, and coherent and that make sense to children?

These questions are really important to consider, though we know we can't address all of them all of the time. Gee was not arguing from a philosophical position, in favor of a traditional or a progressive model of education. He was simply saying, "This is how our kids are choosing to learn," and as teachers, we should learn from them.

Another very important reason that students play online games is that these games enable them to become members of a community. When many veteran teachers were kids, they spent hours in the park, in the fields, or on street corners, playing chasing games, playing marbles, or engaging in mildly transgressive activities such as going down to the riverbank or sneaking into an orchard. In the wonderful *Where Did You Go? Out. What Did You Do? Nothing*, Robert Paul Smith (1957) captured the mildly dangerous adventures of a childhood that was not insulated by overprotective parents and overscheduled music, homework, and sports agendas. In today's world, many parents do not feel that their students will be safe in the park or on the street corner, and as a result, the natural place in which students find an opportunity to socialize is on the Internet. Yes, it can be dangerous, and yes, students will do what they have done for centuries, and construct a private language to make their conversations less transparent to nosy parents. However, as they log onto the Internet the minute they get home from school, most kids have only one aim—to socialize one way or another, and they usually do this with people that they know.

If you look at the following *Pause for Thought*, you will see that Henry, a bright and reasonably well-adjusted 12-year-old who spends many hours a week online, is not avoiding real life by going online. He is participating as a member of an online community, and learning quite a lot while he does so about planning, cooperation, and the history and culture of the world around him and beyond him.

Pause for Thought

What Are Kids Learning from Social Networking, and How Might This Be Useful for Their Teachers?

Question: Why does Henry, an intelligent 12-year-old, get up and spend four hours online on a Saturday morning killing giant chickens?

Answer:

- He was not just killing giant chickens. He was gaining points on a quest.

- Having spent two hours acquiring an Amulet of Glory to enable him to teleport to Camelot, and much of the previous week on a quest to obtain the sword Excalibur from the Lady of the Lake, he was now building up his XP (experience points) to enable him to win a battle against the Black Knight Titan in the realm of the Fisher King.

- After vanquishing the Black Knight, Henry was able to undertake the six or seven subsequent minor tasks that led him to a room containing the Holy Grail. He returned this to King Arthur, and completed the quest.

- All this effort, by the way, was a prelude to undertaking an even more difficult quest—to rescue King Arthur, who has been turned into a statue by Morgan Le Fey.

OK, so Henry is not a bird killer, but a highly motivated nerd?

Wrong again. All the time he was killing chickens, Henry was using the messaging tools in the Runescape© (http://www.runescape.com) to chat with four of his school friends, who were arranging to join forces at an agreed moment to simultaneously attack the King Black Dragon. Good-natured encouragement was followed by exaggerated ridicule when his pals were all duly slain by the dragon.

As teachers, what can we learn from this?

- Quests can be incredibly motivating. Henry's devotion to Runescape© is intermittent, but he's played in bursts for over four years.

- This online game is not antisocial. There is not only friendly coded banter (*noob* = "newbie, new person"), but there is also a great deal of cooperation and sharing of resources, time, and information (players will often take five minutes to lead a "lost" person to safety or will give them "spare" weapons or food, even if they've never met before).

- Henry has learned much from this game about Arthurian legend and medieval life. He also learned much about Greek mythology and ancient civilizations from other games he has played.

Point for reflection and discussion: What are your own views, and those of your colleagues, on your students playing computer games?

The Becta study "Web 2.0 Technologies for Learning at Key Stages 3 and 4" (Crook and Harrison 2008) reported that students between 11 and 16 years old were making extensive use of the social networking opportunities that are often grouped together using the term *Web 2.0*. This rather general term has been used to try to capture the evolution of Web use from passive consumption of content to more active participation, creation, and sharing— to what is sometimes called the *read/write web*. Web 2.0 Internet activities use tools that are broadly concerned with encouraging communication and participation among Internet users, such as blogs, wikis, podcasts, and messaging applications. Three quarters of the 2,600 students surveyed in 2008 had social networking accounts, 78 percent had uploaded content to the Internet (mostly photos or video clips), and the range of personal devices used by students was extensive. However, nearly all Web 2.0 use was outside school, and for social purposes rather than for learning. So it is worth asking two questions about social networking. First, how and why are students using Web 2.0? Second, how are educators beginning to use Web 2.0, and what can we learn from these innovators?

First, here are some statistics. If you add the number of people registered on the three social networking sites most used by teenagers, Bebo®, Habbo®, and Facebook, the total, in July 2013, was over 1.3 billion users (this includes an estimated 8 million Facebook users who falsely claimed to be at least 13 years old when they joined). Therefore, this is not just a passing fad—it's a change in how people live their lives.

Why do students use social networking sites? They seem to offer three important attractions:

- **Communication with friends is easy**. Without having to leave the room, and with a password and one click, they can be in contact with all their friends (and many students have over 1,000 "friends"), exchanging online and offline messages and files.

- **Coordination is easy**. They can plan, scheme, gossip, and exchange information about their mental states, share homework, photos, and plan their lives, all in a space that is (or feels as if it is) parent-free.

- **They can express their personal identities in the way that they want**. They can choose their names, profile photos, and language preferences. In fact, it's a bonus if the way they spell *me nd ma friendzz* drives their parents and teachers to distraction.

All this is well and good. If some of the users of Facebook are reluctant readers, it's really good because poor readers often do not seem to notice that they may be doing quite a lot of reading on the computer, and it is helping to develop their fluency. In the Web 2.0 study, 78 percent of students had not only used email but they also had sent an attachment using email; 87 percent had their own email address; 75 percent had edited a photograph; 53 percent had edited a video; 82 percent had downloaded music from the Internet; 95 percent had watched video online (Crook and Harrison 2008). Older learners engaged more in social networking, while younger learners used the Internet for playing games. For example, the 12 million users of Club Penguin® mostly play very gentle games, and although they can meet their little penguin pals online, they can only engage in the "Ultimate safe chat" by using set phrases from a phrase bank.

Some other statistics from the study that might be helpful for teachers to know are:

- Girls are more likely to own and use a webcam and to record video than boys.

- Boys are significantly more likely to own a gaming device and play more games.

- There is no significant difference between boys and girls with respect to access to MP3 players or mobile phones.

- Social networking and communication activity is more common among girls.

- 15-year-old girls reported significantly greater rates (than did boys) of receiving messages from people they did not know through instant messaging and via email.

Students particularly valued Web 2.0 communication because it was "free." They felt they did not have to pay for the Internet, whereas phone calls and phone text messages were perceived as costing money because usage is usually limited. They also valued it precisely because it did not involve face-to-face contact and could take place when they were in pajamas or had just washed their hair. But one thing was clear: The full use of Web 2.0 for publishing and sharing content was in its infancy. Most students were avid consumers rather than producers of content.

Why Are Some Teachers Already Using Web 2.0, and How Are They Engaging Students?

What the Web 2.0 study team learned was that for a number of teachers, the possibilities of Web 2.0 seemed to harmonize well with modern thinking about educational practice (Crook and Harrison 2008).

In particular, Web 2.0 was felt to:

- offer new opportunities for learners to take more control of their learning and access their own customized information, resources, tools, and services,

- encourage a wider range of expressive capability using multimedia,

- support more collaborative ways of working, community creation, dialogue, and sharing knowledge, and

- offer opportunities for learners' achievements to attract an authentic audience.

How did these opportunities express themselves in the classroom? Initially at least, Web 2.0 was introduced surreptitiously. For example, 13-year-old students in a focus group told us that everyone in their class belonged to Facebook, everyone had a mobile phone, and everyone disobeyed school rules by bringing their phone to school. Access to Facebook was not allowed and was blocked by the school's Internet safety software. This didn't deter the students, however, and every day a cat-and-mouse game was played in which someone brought to school an Internet proxy address which would, at least temporarily, permit access to Facebook, and students texted this address to each other, working on the principle that it would take about a day for the Internet safety team to block that proxy address. The students cast slightly embarrassed glances at their teacher while they were telling us this, but instead of being angry, the teacher smiled and said, "Tell them how you used your proxy address to help me last week." Then, the students told the team that their teacher had been unable to download a picture by Matisse because it was blocked by the school's Internet content filters, and the students had helped her by providing a proxy address so that she could bypass the school's filter system and access the picture. This use was transgressive but ultimately benevolent, as were other students' Web 2.0 activities in school. Students also told the team that they might, for example, use their phone to take a photo of a homework task and email or text it to a friend who was missing the class because of a medical appointment.

Discussion Forums

Discussion forums are online areas, a little like bulletin boards, on which teachers or students can post messages at a time of their own choosing. Most of the Web 2.0 project teachers liked the idea of discussion forums, even if they hadn't created one, and those who had, were pleased with the results. Forums worked best when there had been some prior preparation for the posting task, but once that had been done, discussion boards were felt to be particularly valuable for those students who wrote very slowly, or who tended not to participate in class. They were also good for encouraging peer evaluation and peer comment. Many teachers who used discussion boards also managed to bring in an outside expert (whose commitments might otherwise have made a visit to school impossible), and this could be particularly helpful with students performing above grade level who would benefit from extension activities.

Building a Wiki

A wiki is a Web area that can be developed and edited by a wide range of users. A wiki is, therefore, an ideal locus for a social networking project, provided that the teacher selects a high-quality topic. What is difficult is keeping track of every edit or posting; if every edit needs to be screened or evaluated by the teacher, creating a wiki could be a nightmare. But if the crucial focus is the end product, and everyone is engaged in discussing this, then building a wiki can be a great idea. A wiki is a wonderful example of the new redistribution of authority and knowledge on the Internet, and a teacher can make good use of this and encourage his or her students to be joint creators of knowledge. Not all teachers get this right to begin with. For instance, a language teacher began by introducing a wiki for students to access resources, upload their own work, and hold discussions. However, it quickly became clear that it was becoming quite clogged with discussions, so she moved the discussions to a virtual learning environment where she opened a forum for each piece of work, making it much more manageable.

Voices from the Classroom: How Can You Create a Wiki? features an example of a teacher building a wiki with her students that worked out very well in terms of motivation, participation, and coherence. The task was one that many teachers in the past have given to their students as a face-to-face, whole-class activity: generating a set of rules for how to behave in class. Clearly the challenge here is to avoid this task being carried out as a simple case of "guess what's in the teacher's head." This teacher neatly avoided this pitfall by populating the first draft of the wiki with false rules that would lead to disaster and chaos. The students soon took up the challenge of editing the rules that were present, and with a mixture of class discussion and student participation, they undertook 17 rounds of editing to produce a set of rules that everyone could agree on.

Voices from the Classroom

How Can You Create a Wiki?

How can you create a wiki in a way that will motivate and engage all students?

Below is what one teacher reported to the Web 2.0 team (Crook and Harrison 2008). The teacher was experienced in teaching Information and Communication Technologies (ICT), but what was most important in this lesson was the way she organized two sets of activities: building and editing the wiki and managing the group discussion that deepened the thinking that led into the group editing process.

> One of the first exercises that [the class] did was to compile a wiki. First, I put up some rules, such as:
>
> · You must run around in class.
> · You've got to chew gum.
> · You must spill drinks on the keyboards.
>
> They were all aghast at this, and I said, "Well, you can change it if you like." I showed them how to change a wiki, and after 17 iterations, we'd gotten a set of class rules that I couldn't have bettered myself. So there was that community built up around the wiki...they all felt that they had a choice in what they said and did and that they were able to affect those around them by helping make the rules.

This lesson could be done using Wikipedia® or the free wiki-building tools at http://www.pbworks.com.

Here are some tips for teachers to support the successful use of wikis in the classroom:

- Try to choose a wiki task that has an authentic purpose.

- Encourage, but don't grade, student participation—it's a collective activity.

- Make sure you know how to use all the wiki editing tools.

- Be aware that if you post some inappropriate content as a starter, some creative students will want to continue in the same vein as you; try to suppress your teacherly instincts at this point, and trust the group to put things right.

Can Cell Phones Be Used as a Teaching Tool?

The question of whether mobile phones can be used to support teaching is one that will perhaps appear surprising in 10 years because it is already the case that the mobile phone is beginning to have a major impact on education worldwide.

In 2009, the UK's *Telegraph* newspaper ran a story claiming that the Internet and mobile phones were "damaging education" (Paton 2009). But by the end of 2010, telecommunications experts in the poorest parts of India and Africa were in agreement: the technology that will revolutionize education in the developing world is not the computer—it's the mobile phone. Phones are now delivering English language lessons in Bangladesh, Nigeria, China, and Indonesia, and the content is being tuned to the needs of the learners. Sara Chamberlain, head of interactive content at the BBC World Service Trust, was reported as saying, "In Bangladesh, we have seen how technology—in particular mobiles—can provide quality and affordable education to many millions of people, even if they are living on a few dollars a day" (de Lotbinière 2010). She added that the trust had moved from using British accents to Bangladeshi English because this was the accent the users would need to use to be understood. The BBC had also reduced the length of lessons, lowered the amount of content taught in lessons, and simplified the navigation. The programs were aimed at those with low levels of education, who have dropped out of school, and are not confident in their ability to learn. This initiative, and the reported developments associated with it, sound remarkably in tune with the learning principles outlined by James Gee, and they are, therefore, likely to be enduring.

But international development is not the only area in which education is reaching the mobile phone. Some teachers are experimenting with making short videos of key points in their teaching and posting these on YouTube™ so that their students will be able to download these to their phones if they get stuck with their homework. This is already happening with video clips—there are over 1,000 mini math lessons online on YouTube™, over 5,000 for French, and a similar number for Spanish. For millions of students, these mini-lessons provide "just-in-time" learning at any time of the day or night. Just try typing *How to use the apostrophe* into the YouTube™ search box—there are some great videos out there.

Another new use for mobile phones is for voting. As most teachers know, it's possible for a school to buy a set of "clickers"—classroom voting devices that send an audience response to the speaker or teacher. These interactive voting systems can be brilliant in that they can anonymously tell the teacher whether students have understood a point when they input a multiple choice answer or register their confidence level. The trouble is these systems are expensive, challenging to set up, and time-consuming to give out and collect in. How much simpler, then, to just ask students to text 88886 to say "yes," 88887 to say "no," or 88888 to say "not sure." A similar system is easy to set up if everyone has a computer connected to the Internet. This may sound like a rather traditional teaching method transposed into new technology, but of course, it's up to the teacher to manage the lesson in a traditional or progressive manner. The whole process could be turned over to the students; there is no reason why they should not be the ones drafting the questions and judging the answers. With social networking, the authority position of the teacher is flexible and not a permanent fixture.

Final Thoughts on Capitalizing on What Students Already Know

In this chapter, we have begun to consider some ways in which technology can be introduced into the classroom, often using skills that students and teachers already possess. We haven't looked at software, we haven't looked closely at hardware, and we haven't looked at searching the Internet, supporting weaker readers, or at how technology can support assessment. But we have at least begun to consider the skills that students bring to school, and we have begun to think about how some of these might be used to broaden the range of learning opportunities. In the following *Pause for Thought*, we pose some questions that might help you review some of these opportunities and begin to think about how you might integrate them into your teaching. We strongly encourage you to do this and, if possible, to share your thoughts with a colleague or a friend. After all, that's what social networking is all about!

Pause for Thought

Ideas for the Classroom

Question: Which five classroom ideas presented in this chapter do you think you might like to explore in your own teaching? We invite you to link each idea to the two principles we outlined in the beginning of this chapter:

Principle 1: Make students your co-workers, and build upon their expertise.

Principle 2: Integrate technology into a piece of teaching in which you are already an expert so that the pedagogy is not dramatically different from your regular practice.

What are some of the possibilities?

- "We teach one another now"—give students the chance to teach one another and you.

- Give the students (some of) your plans—what would they choose to do?

- Have students make an "I can…" list and conduct an audit of their skills.

- Publish students' "I can…" charts so that everyone knows how much knowledge is held by the group.

- Have students interview one anther to find out about their cooperative gaming skills.

- Offer a multimedia task instead of a written one.

- Offer more of a range of learning styles, technologies, and tasks.

- Have students compile a glossary of their Facebook language in a wiki.

- Incorporate a quest into your teaching.

- Bring a discussion board into your teaching and have students police it.

- Encourage Web publication for a wider and more authentic audience.

- Publish a mini-video on a school website or on YouTube™.

- Have students publish a mini-video on a school website or on YouTube™.

- Run an electronic voting lesson with an authentic purpose for anonymity.

If you try out some of these activities, please try to share the outcomes with a colleague or a friend. What worked well? Why? What needs to change?

Questions for Reflection

1. Your authors have suggested two principles: making your students co-workers in developing technology use, and integrating technology into things that you already do. Can you think of a third principle that you would want to have to guide your own professional development?

2. In what ways can you make use of the different knowledge and skills that boys and girls possess in relation to technology use?

3. Select a new idea that you would like to try from this chapter. What procedures do you need to have in place in order to implement this idea? Once you've tried the ideas, share what you've learned with a colleague.

CHAPTER 3

Strategies for Using Digital Tools to Support Literacy Development

In this chapter, you will learn:

- how the principles underpinning the Universal Design for Learning (UDL) framework support the diverse needs of students in your classroom; and

- how digital tools can support literacy development for your students.

After reading this chapter, you will:

- know strategies to develop reading vocabulary using digital tools for literacy;

- understand strategies to develop reading fluency using digital tools for literacy;

- know strategies to promote wide reading using digitized texts; and

- be able to differentiate instruction using digital tools for diverse populations in the classroom.

As educators, we are rightly concerned that issues of equity, social justice, and equality of opportunity permeate all that we do in schools to support the diverse cultural, linguistic, and learning needs of our students in order to help them achieve their potential and participate fully in society within a global community. We know, for example, that the number of struggling readers in our classrooms is growing and that the number of students for whom the home language is not the language of instruction in school is increasing (Biancarosa and Snow 2006; Crawford 2004). Our school curricula have tended toward supporting the mythical "average" student in the classroom in a one-size-fits-all approach, and we have then, with varying degrees of success, "fixed" the curriculum to support the needs of struggling readers, English Language Learners (ELL), and students who are academically gifted. The Universal Design for Learning (UDL) (Rose and Meyer 2002) framework is based on the principle that the design of curriculum should anticipate the needs of all learners from the outset rather than be "fixed" later for students with diverse learning needs. The framework was inspired by the "universal design for all" concept in architecture where buildings are designed from the outset to accommodate the needs of diverse populations. Similarly, a UDL curriculum minimizes barriers to learning and maximizes support for students so that the ensuing curriculum is flexible, supportive, and responsive to the learning needs of all students (Hall, Strangman, and Meyer 2003).

The principles underpinning UDL are helpful to us as we consider, in this chapter, the possibilities that technology affords us to support all of our students on the journey to becoming better readers, writers, communicators, collaborators, thinkers, and, ultimately, lifelong learners. These principles are presented in the sections that follow.

Principle 1: To support students' recognition networks and provide multiple examples and means of representation.

- Assess prior student knowledge and scaffold student learning.

- Customize the display of information by presenting it in different modalities (e.g., text size, font, color, video, audio) to reduce barriers to learning.

Principle 2: To support students' strategic networks and provide multiple means of action and expression.

- Provide multiple means of expression, communication, and fluency development within a cognitive apprenticeship framework.

- Provide guided, ongoing, and flexible support.

Principle 3: To support students' affective networks provide multiple means of engagement.

- Offer options to develop and sustain interest and optimize choice.

- Provide authentic learning opportunities and adjustable levels of challenge.

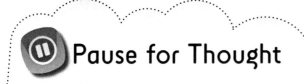

Pause for Thought

Integrating Technology, Content, and Pedagogy

Borrowing from Ito and her colleagues' great title *Hanging Out, Messing Around and Geeking Out: Kids Living and Learning With New Media* (2010), we would urge you to take time to *hang out* and play with the range of digital tools described in this chapter on a Saturday afternoon or other free time. Showcase your learning at an Internet party! Make time to *mess around* with technology by teaching colleagues to consider the possibilities these digital tools have for enhancing literacy in your classroom. Then, *geek out* with your colleagues to discuss how you could repurpose these digital tools in appropriate and creative ways to design a literacy curriculum to integrate technology, content, and pedagogical knowledge (Mishra and Koehler 2006).

Digital tools offer the potential to promote motivation and engagement and to support the diverse needs of all of our students by creating "scaffolded learning environments where supports can be adjusted in relation to students' needs and preferences" (Dalton 2008, 155). For example, digital tools can provide:

- multiple media formats, such as video, audio, and image supports;

- opportunities to practice skills and strategies with assistance;

- possibilities for highlighting critical features of texts;

- support for receptive processes through, for example, text-to-speech (TTS) functionality;

- opportunities to demonstrate new knowledge and learning through multiple modes of presentation;

- adjustable levels of challenge;

- choice of content and tools; and

- ongoing assessment opportunities.

In this chapter, we consider the ways in which digital tools can be harnessed to build literacy in the curriculum in the areas of *developing reading vocabulary*, *promoting reading fluency*, and engaging our students in *digitized reading environments*.

 ## Common Core to the Fore

Helping Students Become College and Career Ready

The CCSS focus on skills such as problem solving, collaboration, and fluency with technology. These standards call attention to the skills requisite for any nation's workforce that strives to be competitive in the 21st century. Guiding students to acquire these competencies can no longer be an ancillary aim—it is an economic and social imperative that is central to civic participation. However, teaching them is not only difficult, but it also represents a significant shift for most classroom teachers. Most of us are tentative about ways to use technology to support and extend learning, but taking small steps in doing so offers big rewards in terms of students' engagement and investment in learning. Creating an environment that ensures that students are prepared to strategically use a variety of technologies is central to the aims of the CCSS and is an important target for schools.

Vocabulary knowledge is important for success in reading, writing, and ultimately learning in school. Research suggests that children from high-poverty school districts enter school with vocabularies that are smaller than their more affluent peers (Graves 2006). The section that follows considers what we know about effective vocabulary instruction. Following this, we consider how digital tools can be utilized to advance both receptive and generative processes in vocabulary development.

What Do We Know about Effective Vocabulary Instruction?

Effective vocabulary instruction:

- teaches important words and word learning strategies (Graves 2006).

- promotes wide reading and incidental learning opportunities and involves lots of rich discussion and talk about text and experiences (Anderson and Nagy 1992).

- recognizes that word learning is incremental—word knowledge builds over time through rich, repeated, and varied exposure and use in authentic contexts (Beck, McKeown, and Kucan 2002).

- helps students to become independent word learners (Blachowicz and Fisher 2004).

- fosters word consciousness and word play (Scott and Nagy 2004).

- views words as networks of concepts and teaches conceptually related words in meaningful contexts (Nagy and Scott 2000).

Digital tools can support both receptive and generative processes to enhance vocabulary development (Castek, Dalton, and Grisham 2012). In the sections that follow, we consider a range of digital tools to support word learning and vocabulary development in the following areas:

- Using word cloud generators such as Wordle™, Tagxedo, and WordSift for graphical representations of text

- Generating vocabulary videos to promote social learning and foster word consciousness

- Creating tutorials using, for example, Show Me, to promote word-learning strategies

- Utilizing collaborative learning tools, such as VoiceThread and Thinglink

Graphical Representations of Text

Word Clouds

Word clouds are graphical representations of inputted text and can be created in Wordle™ (http://www.wordle.net/) or Tagxedo (http://www.tagxedo.com/). The frequency of words in a particular text is reflected in the size of the words in the word cloud. Simply copy and paste an Internet URL or the text from a word processing document into the *Create* section on either Wordle™ or Tagxedo. Word clouds can be presented in different layouts, fonts, colors, and organization. Save the word cloud as an image, and you can display it on your interactive whiteboard, embed it on a class wiki, post it on the class blog, or print it for use in the classroom.

Some Possible Uses for Word Clouds in the Classroom

Examples of how we have used word clouds in the classroom include:

- **Have students create collaborative word clouds**, where a number of students input and edit text collaboratively, using Google Docs™ (https://docs.google.com) or TitanPad (http://titanpad.com/ref). For example, have students generate a list of synonyms, contractions, or tricky words and input them into a word cloud generator (see Figure 3.1 for a *Tricky Words* word cloud). The more the word is repeated in a text, the greater the size of that word in the word cloud. To connect words in a word cloud (e.g. the contraction *is not~isn't*), place a tilde (~) between the words you wish to connect.

- **Use word clouds before, during, and after reading.** For example, input text excerpts into a word-cloud generator and have students make predictions or analyze character traits based on the word cloud. See Figure 3.2 for a word cloud for *Charlotte's Web* (E. B. White 1952). At a glance, you can see the tenor and subject matter of a text at a macro level.

Figure 3.1 Tricky Words Word Cloud (Created in Wordle™)

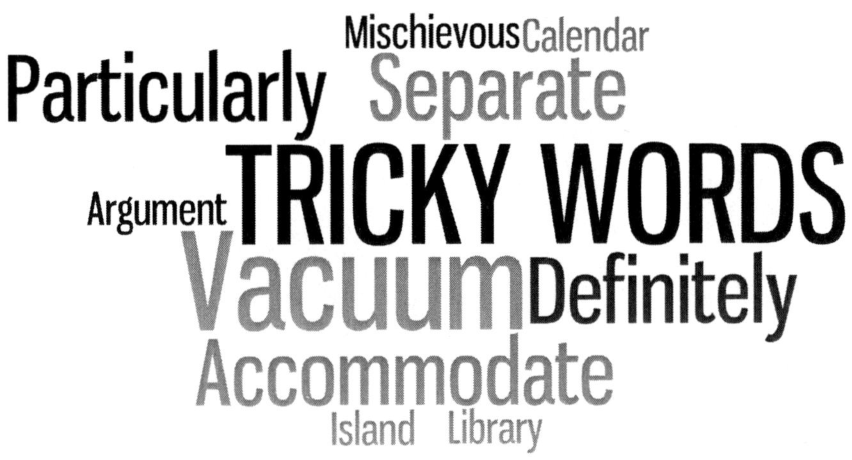

MischievousCalendar
Particularly Separate
Argument TRICKY WORDS
VacuumDefinitely
Accommodate
Island Library

Printed with permission from Bernadette Dwyer

Figure 3.2 *Charlotte's Web* Word Cloud (Created in Wordle™)

Printed with permission from Bernadette Dwyer

- **Word clouds can also be used for Internet inquiry**. For example, do an Internet search and then copy and paste the text from the first page of the returned search results screen into a word-cloud generator Show students the word cloud and ask them to identify the key search terms that were used in the search.

A simple key word search for uses of Wordle™ or Tagxedo in the classroom will provide numerous other examples. Why not discuss the possibilities for using word clouds for vocabulary development with your teaching colleagues and brainstorm a list together?

WordSift

WordSift (http://www.wordsift.com) is a teaching tool to sift vocabulary in a text. WordSift captures an inputted text and can do the following:

- Display the most frequent words in text in a variety of formats (in alphabetical order, from frequent to rare, or from social studies, mathematics, language arts, etc.)

- Present Google™ images and a visual thesaurus of highlighted words

- Provide examples of selected vocabulary within the context of the sentences from the original text

You can copy a URL, text from a website, or a class text and paste it into WordSift. The WordSift program instantly tags and identifies the important words within the text and creates a word cloud of these words. Text size indicates the frequency of the words in the text. A visual thesaurus is also displayed for words that the teacher selects. A web of words shows the network of meaning between words. This helps the reader to activate prior knowledge and create associations between words. The highlighted words are also displayed within the original text. In Figure 3.3, we have captured the text of the "I Have a Dream" speech by Dr. Martin Luther King Jr. and have input it into WordSift. In Figure 3.4, you can see the sifted text displaying the most frequent words in the text. We have chosen the word *dream* from the text, and you can see Google™ images for the word and a visual thesaurus displaying a web of words related to the chosen word. The highlighted word *dream* is also shown within the context of the sentences in the original text. Watch a WordSift demonstration on YouTube™ (see Appendix B for URL).

Providing multiple representations of vocabulary, whether in images, context, or word clouds, provides support for struggling readers and English language learners as they grapple with complex text in the classroom.

Figure 3.3 WordSift Screen for Text of the "I Have a Dream" Speech by Dr. Martin Luther King Jr.

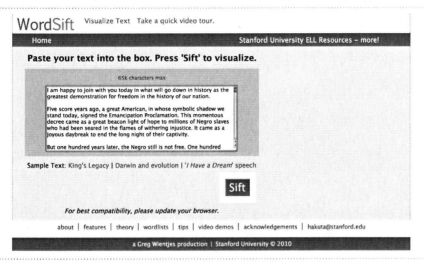

Printed with permission from WordSift

Figure 3.4 Completed WordSift for text of the "I Have a Dream" Speech by Dr. Martin Luther King Jr.

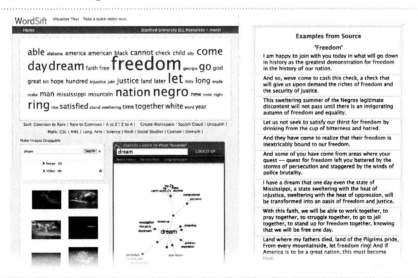

Printed with permission from WordSift

Vocabulary Videos to Promote Social Learning and Foster Word Consciousness

Vocabulary videos are short (about 45 seconds long) videos that are produced by groups of students, thus promoting the social nature of language learning. The use of a range of multimedia supports enhances both the depth and breadth of vocabulary development and promotes both generative and receptive processes.

On the *Literacy Beat Blog* (to which both Bernadette Dwyer and Jill Castek contribute), Bridget Dalton has blogged about the ways in which her students have created vocabulary videos. The link to read her post to view examples can be found in Appendix B.

Vocabulary videos can be produced in different ways that include a small digital camcorder, a tablet device, a high-definition camera, or a smartphone.

Creating a Vocabulary Video

1. Provide models of vocabulary videos for your students. See these examples:

    -   **Scientifically Speaking** (Figure 3.5) A series of video episodes investigating the origins of words for content areas. They were created in iMovie® by Nick Mitchell and Katrina Theilman. See an example of the episode on *transmit, absorb,* and *reflect* at http://vimeo.com/42777257.
    -   **Vocabahead** (Figure 3.6) Over 1,000 words explained using short cartoon style videos. Vocabulary is based on SAT tests. See for example, the explanation of *rescind* at http://www.vocabahead.com/. Vocabahead is also available for free as an app for iPad® or Android™ devices.
    -   **Vocab Videos** See the examples created by Bridget Dalton's students on YouTube™. A URL for the videos can be found in Appendix B.

Figure 3.5 Screen Capture of Vocabulary Video from Scientifically Speaking

Printed with permission from Katrina Theilman

Figure 3.6 Screen Capture From Vocabahead Showing Featured Word *Overwrought*

Printed with permission from VocabAhead

2. Choose Tier 2 words (Beck, McKeown, and Kucan 2002), which are sophisticated ways of saying everyday words (e.g., *uttered* instead of *said*), or Tier 3 words, which are related to a particular discipline like science or mathematics. Alternatively, you could use words from the Vocabahead website (http://www.vocabahead.com) or from a novel students are studying, or allow students to choose the words.

3. Have students work in small groups, of two or three, to brainstorm synonyms for the focus word. After they make their own list of synonyms, students can use the thesaurus in a word-processing program or an online thesaurus to generate additional synonyms. Have students deepen their knowledge of the word by discussing issues such as how the word is used, who might use it, why it is used, and in what contexts it is used.

4. Following discussion, have students plan a script based on the focus word in which the focus word and synonyms for that word are used multiple times. Then, provide cameras and have them film a short improvised skit (45–60 seconds duration). Have a short film festival during which students present their short films to the class for discussion. It is also possible to publish the videos to YouTube™, Teachertube®, and other online video-sharing platforms. Make sure you have permissions for publication from your students and/or parents before uploading.

Creating Tutorials to Promote Word-Learning Strategies: ShowMe

ShowMe (http://www.showme.com) is a free, downloadable app from the iTunes® store for creating tutorials to share with your students. You can record a voice-over and create and draw on the iPad®, recreating explanations and demonstrations from your lessons. Students can view and listen to explanations from your lessons on their own time and at their own pace in an example of the "flipped classroom." In addition, you can publish your tutorials to the ShowMe learning community. ShowMe also has generative possibilities. For example, students could design and create ShowMe artifacts of vocabulary learning for homonyms or synonyms (Castek and Tilson 2012). Student-created examples can be found by searching "multiple meaning words" within ShowMe (see Appendix B for URL).

Bringing It Together: Utilizing Collaborative Learning Tools

Digital tools can be used to promote collaborative learning opportunities in the classroom. In the sections that follow, we describe how VoiceThread® and Thinglink can be used to enhance literacy development.

VoiceThread

VoiceThread® for educators (http://ed.voicethread.com) provides an interactive online forum for conversations and student collaboration. VoiceThreads® are collaborative multimedia slide shows that integrate images, documents, and sound files (a link to Online tutorials for creating a VoiceThread® can be found in Appendix B). VoiceThreads® allow for anytime, anywhere, asynchronous conversations, and allow participants to annotate and comment in five different ways: using voice (via a microphone), text (using a keyboard), audio file, video (with a Web cam), or annotation through doodling. Participants click on *Record* or *Type* to add a comment, which then appears around the border of the image, slide, or video. Teachers can create accounts for their students. Images or avatars (for example, created with Doppelme) of the participants are added to the accounts. The interplay of multimedia and commentary are essential parts of the process and encourage student response. VoiceThread® can be used to discuss the artifacts produced by the digital tools discussed in the chapter thus far to reinforce word learning and enhance vocabulary development.

At Voicethread4education, you can view 26 different ways to use VoiceThread® in the classroom. (See Appendix B for the URL.) Here are some of our favorites from the list for language arts:

- **#1 Mystery Scene:** Provide students with a mystery scene or an image and ask them what is happening and what might have caused it. What vocabulary can be used to describe the scene?

- **#5 Video:** Ask students to view, comment on, and review a short video. For example, have them comment on one of the vocabulary videos produced by the class group.

- **#7 Novel:** Have students comment on a character or a protagonist from a novel.

- **#10 Inferencing:** Provide an intriguing image with people in it, and ask students to comment on what the people in the image might be thinking. This would be useful for developing inferencing strategies and reinforcing vocabulary.

- **#14 Digital Portfolio:** Students can create a digital portfolio using images, video, and text.

Thinglink

Thinglink is a digital tool that allows students to explore topics through collaborative discussions. Students can insert interactive links to tag an image by adding pop-up multimedia hot spots. Hot spots can link to music, audio files, video, descriptions, definitions, or quotations.

Figure 3.7 Thinglink Showing Featured Word *Perseverance*

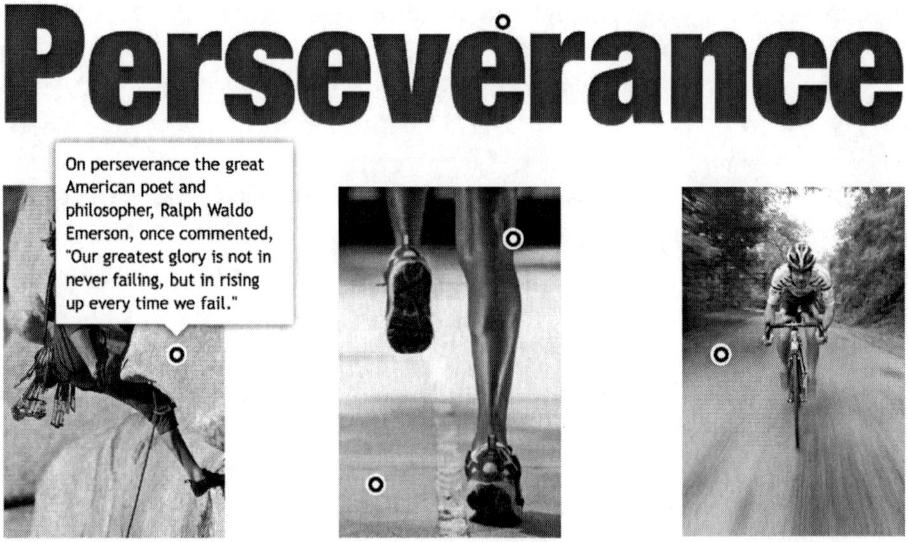

> On perseverance the great American poet and philosopher, Ralph Waldo Emerson, once commented, "Our greatest glory is not in never failing, but in rising up every time we fail."

Printed with permission from Donna Baumbach and @SalilWilson

In the Thinglink example in Figure 3.7, images were added to illustrate the target word *perseverance*. (See Appendix B for a URL for more examples.) This was combined with a dictionary definition, a quotation using the word (as shown in the figure), and a short video showing how people from a range of backgrounds (sports, music, politicians) persevered against the odds. You

58

could also add examples of the target word used in context, an audio file to aid pronunciation (great for English language learners), and vocabulary videos to illustrate usage (discussed earlier in the chapter). Students could create photo collages in Photovisi (http://www.photovisi.com) to tag each image with a pop-up of descriptive adjectives, synonyms, or antonyms.

Thus far, we have looked at how digital tools can be used to enhance the development of reading vocabulary in both receptive and generative ways. We have explored how word clouds present graphical representations of text; how vocabulary videos promote social learning in tandem with fostering word consciousness; how we can use tutorials to advance word learning strategies; and how collaborative learning tools can be used to encourage discussion about word knowledge. Next, we turn our attention to using digital tools to develop reading fluency.

Developing Reading Fluency Using Digitized Texts

Reading fluency has been referred to as the "neglected reading goal" (Allington 1983). However, the National Reading Panel report (NICHHD 2000) found that there was persuasive and ample evidence to support the place of reading fluency as an essential component of the classroom curriculum literacy program.

What Do We Know about Developing Reading Fluency?

- Reading fluency has been defined as "efficient, effective word recognition skills that permit a reader to construct the meaning of text" (Pikulski and Chard 2005, 510).

- Reading fluency comprises interplay between automatic word recognition and expression in reading (Rasinski and Samuels 2011). A fluent reader reads expressively and meaningfully as well as accurately and at the right speed.

- The relationship between word recognition, reading fluency, and reading comprehension is complex. We know that word recognition and reading fluency enable the development of reading comprehension, yet they are not synonymous with it. As educators, we have all encountered students who are "word callers"—students who read the words in the text speedily and accurately and yet, when asked, have no idea of the gist of the text and are unable to recall or summarize the content of what they have read.

- When readers can decode words fluently, they have more cognitive energy to focus on understanding what they are reading as they construct meaning from text (LaBerge and Samuels 1974).

- Effective instruction in the development of reading fluency should incorporate a synergy between modeling, assisted reading, practice, and phrasing (Rasinski and Samuels 2011).

Good readers read appropriate levels of text, are given more opportunities to read silently, are encouraged to self-monitor, and are urged to use multiple strategies when meaning breaks down. Struggling readers, on the other hand, read text that is often too difficult for them, are asked to read orally (often in round-robin type scenarios), are interrupted more by the teacher and are encouraged to decode or sound out words as a dominant reading strategy (Allington 2001).

The use of digital tools offers struggling readers and English language learner students multiple ways to develop reading fluency and listening comprehension. It also provides access pathways to difficult text through multimodal representations.

In the sections that follow, we consider ways in which digital technologies can support the development of reading fluency through modeling, assisted reading, phrasing, and wide reading in ways that encourage receptive, expressive, and generative processes.

Using Audio Recording to Develop Reading Fluency

Audio recordings can be created simply by using a digital voice recorder or an MP3 player or, more elaborately by using websites such as Podbean, Audacity®, or Garage Band® (see Appendix B for URLs).

Audio recordings of text can be used to support receptive, generative, and expressive processes for

- developing listening comprehension;

- repeated and assisted reading of text; and

- providing a model of fluent reading.

Strategies for Using Audio Recordings for Developing Listening Comprehension

Have students listen to and evaluate audio recordings of fluent reading or speaking. You can create audio recordings yourself or download podcasts from the Internet. As students listen individually to a recording for the first time, have them consider the following questions (adapted from Hertzberg 2012):

- What do I hear, see, feel, taste, or smell as I listen?

- What image do I see in my head? How has the author created this image?

Have students listen to the recording again and Think-Pair-Share, using the following questions:

- What images were created by the recording? Can you re-create the text as a visualization in a drawing?

- What words were interesting in the text? What words would cause difficulty for a friend (Pearson 2006)?

- How was the text read? Did the reader pause at suitable points? Was the text read expressively? Did the reader read at an appropriate rate?

Strategies for Using Audio Recording to Enable Repeated Reading and Practice

Multiple readings of the same text support students in developing intonation, expression, phrasing, and reading rate, an important process according to the Common Core State Standards (NCCS 2010). Provide students with explicit instruction and modeling in what we call R5—*rehearse, record, review, rewind,* and *redo.* First, have students *rehearse,* reading a passage individually from a selected text. Next, direct students to *record* themselves reading the passage using a digital-recording device. Have students, working in pairs, provide feedback to one another in the form of "Buddy Listening." Have each student listen attentively to his or her partner's recording and provide feedback to *review* the reading. Provide a checklist-style recording sheet that shows, for example, the number of errors made, the expression of the reading, attention to punctuation, and reading rate for students to complete. Then, have students *rewind* the process to reread and record the same passage again. Finally, direct students to listen again and *redo* an evaluation of reading fluency. Each stage in the R5 procedure—*rehearse, record, review, rewind,* and *redo*—provides opportunities for multiple readings of the same passage and helps students to evaluate their reading fluency with partner support.

We have considered ways to develop reading fluency that support receptive, generative, and expressive processes. These included using digital tools for developing listening comprehension, modeling, repeated reading, and assisted reading of text. In the final section of the chapter, we consider ways in which digitized texts can foster reading engagement and promote reading development through wide reading.

Other strategies for providing opportunities for practice to develop reading fluency include:

- **Readers Theater:** Readers theater is a fun and effective way for students to practice multiple readings of a text. No props are needed, although younger readers may enjoy using masks of the characters from the text. Scripts for readers theater may be sourced online from:
  - www.readinglady.com
  - www.aaronshep.com/rt/index.html
  - www.readingonline.org/electronic/elec_index.asp?HREF=carrick/index.html
  - www.timelessteacherstuff.com

- **TV Captioning:** Turning on the captioning function on a television is a way of transforming what can often be a rather passive activity into an active activity. Students develop reading fluency as they read captions from their favorite programs.

Using Digitized Texts for Reading Development

"The more that you read, the more things you will know. The more that you learn, the more places you'll go." The wisdom of Dr. Seuss reverberates in this quotation from *I Can Read With My Eyes Shut!* (1978). There is ample evidence that engagement with reading and frequent reading are associated with success in reading and increased reading attainment (e.g., Guthrie and Wigfield 2000). Digital texts offer possibilities for motivating and engaging readers through a range of inbuilt tools. Popular devices for digital texts, at the time of this writing, include the Kindle™ (Amazon), the Nook® (Barnes and Noble), the EReader™ (Sony), iPad® (Apple) and other Android™ tablet devices (e.g., Samsung Galaxy Note™). Digital texts can encourage both receptive and generative processes. In the sections that follow, we discuss the opportunities offered by digitized texts.

Digitized texts introduce a number of possibilities for learner control to support literacy development. Scaffolds are embedded in the texts to both enhance access to texts and enable the construction of meaning for a range of diverse learners, such as struggling readers or English language learners. Embedded supports introduce physicality to the interaction between text and reader.

Digitized texts offer two key supports to individualize the reading experience:

- **Text-to-Speech Functionality:** Text-to-speech supports enable students to bypass the decoding bottleneck which helps enhance their listening comprehension and develops automaticity in reading fluency and word recognition. Studies have shown variance in the effectiveness of such supports because, in terms of self-regulation, students over- or under-utilize them (Dalton and Strangman 2006).

- **Inbuilt Digital Tools:** Digitized texts allow readers to manipulate font size. They can also include an inbuilt text-to-speech functionality, highlighter, dictionary, and glossary. Digitized texts allow readers to physically interact with the text through digital notes in the form of *thinkmarks*. Thinkmarks encourage reader response and allow readers to record fleeting thoughts as they make connections, ask questions of the text, and focus on vocabulary within the text.

For more information about the affordance of digital text and implementing ideas in your classroom, see Chapter 4, *Strategies for Using eReaders and Digital Books to Expand the Reading Experience.*

Digitized Texts Available on the Internet

- **eBooks** are also becoming more widely available from local public libraries.

- **Explor-eBook**, winner of the 2013 TCA award, is a collection of content-area books that can be quickly and easily downloaded on the Web, desktop computers (PC), iPads®, or Android™ tablets. No subscription is required to use Explor-eBook. Enhanced eBook features include bookmarks, thumbnail navigation, keyword search, and pop-up glossaries. (See Appendix B for URL.)

- **Project Gutenberg** has over 40,000 books in digitized format, which can be downloaded to computer or mobile devices (see Appendix B for URL). A search for students' literature revealed a range of students' classics by authors such as Charles Dickens, Oscar Wilde, Anna Sewell, and Kenneth Grahame.

- **Storyline Online** features members of the Screen Actors Guild reading favorite students' books aloud (see Appendix B for URL).

- **Tumblebooks** is a collection of licensed titles from students' book publishers. Tumblebooks offers a free trial for 30 days (see Appendix B for URL).

A number of websites offer educational resources in multiple languages such as English, Spanish, and Portuguese. This supports English language learners as they make intertextual connections between their primary and secondary language resources to build cognitive flexibility and metalinguistic awareness.

- **The International Children's Digital Library** has over 2,880 books available in 48 different languages for free (see Appendix B for URL). The simple search feature makes it easy to find books that match the age range and interest level of all students. For English language learners, the site includes a feature that allows the reader to switch the language for instant translation.

- **Monterey Bay Aquarium** provides a delightful eBook about sea otters called *Pup's Supper/La Cena del Cachorro* (see Appendix B for URL).

- **NASA's Sun-Earth Day Multimedia Students' Books** are interactive multimedia texts accessible in both English and Spanish (see Appendix B for URL). Each book poses essential questions and presents concepts that help students address them. Related resources, such as an image gallery and a dictionary, extend ideas presented in the text.

- **The Rainforest Alliance Virtual Story Books** are available in English, Spanish, and Portuguese (see Appendix B for URL). Exploring these engaging texts extends emergent bilingual students' comprehension and vocabulary while helping make connections between languages.

- **Storyline Online** Members of the screen actors guild conduct a read-aloud of favorite children's books (see Appendix B for URL).

Creating and Producing Digitized Texts in the Classroom: Book Builder

Book Builder from the Center for Applied Special Technology (CAST) (http://bookbuilder.cast.org/) offers a supported digital reading environment and is underpinned by principles of universal design for learning (Rose and Meyer 2002). Book Builder is easy to use, with a comprehensive *How to Tips* and *Resources* pages. One of our favorite books on the CAST website is *Play Ball with Me! A Joel and Angel Book*, written and illustrated by Anne Meyer. The digital book features Anne's two dogs in a story of the trials of friendship, and is beautifully illustrated by her own digital photographs of her two charming dogs (see Figure 3.8). The book contains audio links and a helpful illustrated glossary of terms. It features a text-to-speech functionality but develops more than just listening comprehension.

Figure 3.8 Illustration from *Play Ball With Me!*

Printed with permission from cast.org

One of the strengths of Book Builder is the presence of avatar coaches, such as Percie, Emo, and Can-Do. These coaches can be customized to the learning needs of your students. Each coach can help readers develop response, expand vocabulary, and build strategy usage (e.g., making predictions, forging connections, asking questions). Students can also craft their own responses to answer teacher provided questions. A customized reading environment affirms the uniqueness of the child as a reader, a writer, and a thinker. Teachers can create free accounts for themselves and their students on the website. Children can also create their own eBooks using the Book Builder tools. Books can also be created in multiple languages to support the needs of English language learners.

Common Core to the Fore

Using Digital Tools to Enhance Reading Development

The Common Core State Standards provide an overview of capacities of 21st century literate individuals. These new standards assert that students should be able to use technology and digital media strategically and capably.

Classroom Connection

Bringing It Together: Turning Over a New Leaf as Book Builder Meets the Language Experience Approach

Katie Murphy has successfully used the Language Experience Approach (LEA) with her first-grade students to develop early literacy skills and promote reading engagement. She likes the fact that LEA builds on the linguistic knowledge, shared experiences, and cultural backgrounds of her students. Typically, LEA incorporates a number of sequenced steps that include shared class experience, class discussion of experience, dictation and recording the experience, shared and individual reading of the text, and building early literacy skills using the LEA story. LEA was developed in the 1960s, and this year, Katie has been considering the possibilities for updating this approach by integrating digital tools with LEA. Here's what Digital LEA with multimodal supports looks like in the classroom (drawing on Labbo, Eakle, and Montero 2002; Ryan 2012).

- **Shared Experience.** A Visit from the Fire Brigade to the School. Katie had invited the local fire department to visit the school. The first graders waited in the schoolyard and were dizzy with excitement when the fire department and local firefighters arrived. The firefighters talked about their experiences and the students got to wear the hats and uniforms of the firefighters, try out the fire hoses, and sit in the fire engine. They recorded the experience using digital and flip cameras.

- **Discussion of Experience.** Back in the classroom, students worked in groups to discuss their experiences of the visit and to view and sequence the digital photographs they had taken. Later, they discussed the experience as a whole-class activity. Katie asked probing questions to promote vocabulary development.

- **Dictation and Recording Experience.** Following the discussion, Katie moved to her laptop (connected to the interactive whiteboard) and had students dictate sentences to represent the story of their experience while she recorded each sentence in a Word file. Next, they discussed the vocabulary in the created story. Katie asked students, "What words would cause difficulty for a friend?" She recorded the words students chose as difficult. She then asked, "Can we think of more sophisticated ways of saying some of the words we used?" Students accessed an online thesaurus and used a Think-Pair-Share strategy to retrieve synonyms for the words used in the story. Later, Katie used BookBuilder to develop each page of the story using the digital images captured by the students. She then added an audio recording of the text to each page. Using the words students chose as difficult and the synonyms they found, she created the glossary of terms with images, audio helps, and context sentences.

- **Choral Reading of Text.** The next day, students listened to the recording of the story and viewed the story in BookBuilder as Katie showed it on her interactive whiteboard. Then, they read along with the digitized text as a choral reading of the text to develop reading fluency. Next, individual students volunteered to read sentences from the story.

- **Developing Literacy Skills.** Katie chose early literacy skills to work with in the story, such as concepts of print, phonological awareness, phonics, and vocabulary. For example, she used iCard Sort for iPad® to sift vocabulary words into word families. Then, she grouped the students and encouraged them to generate questions. Katie had previously modeled and demonstrated the difference between thick questions (higher order) requiring multiple answers, and thin questions (lower order) requiring a yes/no or single answer. She encouraged students to make connections: text-to-self connections, text-to-text connections, and text-to-world connections. Students thought carefully about asking questions and making connections as they knew their teacher would select some of these questions and connections for avatars such as Percie, Emo, and Can-Do, which would be added to their story.

- **Publishing the Digitized Story.** When the story was completed, the students read it on class laptops or tablets and wrote their thoughts directly onto the digitized book in student response areas of the text. Later, the story was published onto the BookBuilder website, and students read the story at home with their parents, older siblings, or other family members.

- **Next Steps for Digitized LEA with Multimodal Supports.** Next semester, Katie is going to use BookBuilder to create informational texts with hyperlinks to carefully selected videos. She is also considering linking to VoiceThread®, where students can add text, images, video, and audio to enhance discussions about each book.

Final Thoughts on the Discussion of Digital Tools for Literacy Development

In this chapter, we explored several resources and ideas that support students' literacy development through the use of online tools and resources. In the chapters that follow, we'll go on to discuss some of the more unique aspects of online reading and writing as students explore online information and compose texts in online and socially-networked Internet spaces.

Questions for Reflection

1. How can digital tools advance the principles of Universal Design for Learning in the classroom?

2. How can digital tools be used to differentiate instruction for diverse populations in the classroom?

3. In collaboration with your teaching colleagues, take time to delve deeper into the features of the range of digital tools explored in the chapter. You can perhaps focus on one area to begin with, like vocabulary development, reading fluency, or using digitized texts. Showcase your learning at an Internet party. Consider with colleagues how these digital tools can support curriculum content, classroom pedagogies, and learning in the classroom.

Strategies for Using eReaders and Digital Books to Expand the Reading Experience

In this chapter, you will learn:

- what specific supports eReaders make available to students to enhance their reading experience;

- how these supports can be benefical for students' reading development; and

- ideas and tools for creating eBooks with your students.

After reading this chapter, you will be prepared to:

- evaluate the characteristics of eTexts to determine which are best for your students;

- use available eReader technologies to expand students' access and engagement with electronic texts; and

- organize classroom reading activities to support the collaborative reading experiences that are made possible by eReading technologies.

The last few years have seen a multitude of eReaders spring up. They are described by terms such as *eBooks*, *eTexts*, *eReaders*, and *digital texts*. These terms are not always clearly and consistently defined, in part because of the rapidly changing nature of the technology itself. The terms *digital book* and *eBook* are often used interchangeably, although some consider an eBook to be static and a digital book to have multimedia elements, such as sound or interactive elements. Along with terminology, formats of digital books may vary. Traditional digital books are books published first in print and then reconfigured into a digital design. An original digital book is meant to be read on a digital device, with no corresponding print-book format. (For URLs to find examples of digital texts, see Appendix B.)

The recent availability of electronic books has shifted what the experience of reading a book looks like and feels like. The latest eReaders offer a reading experience that parallels the affordances of the printed book, but with additional enhancements such as wireless connectivity and storage that make it feasible for devices to hold more than 1,000 titles that can be accessed on demand. However, eReading technologies remain primarily targeted at motivated, proficient readers, who are reading recreationally for non-educational purposes. Whatever the purpose for choosing to use digital books with students, care should be given to selecting books with multimedia elements that deepen the reader's understanding and appreciation of the story rather than distract from the meaning of the text. In Figures 4.1, Beth Dobler and Daniel Donahoo, elementary school teachers, offer an insightful set of criteria, set up as a rubric, to help you reflect on what makes a high-quality digital book. (Visit Beth's Dobler's post on the Literacy Beat Blog titled *Let the Reader Beware: Evaluating Digital Books*. See Appendix B for URL). In this post, she reflects on the ways digital books and their incorporation of multimedia elements, including text, images, music, sound effects, and narration, can be both motivating and distracting to readers.) The rubric in Figure 4.1 can be used to help you choose quality digital books.

Many eReading technologies are just beginning to emerge as classroom tools with the inclusion of new features that have the potential to change the way readers interface with eTexts. An exciting potential exists for these new eReading technologies to respond to both the changing demands of school curricula as well as the changing needs of students, especially those who require additional support. Digital texts in eBook form offer the possibility of "scaffolded digital reading" (Dalton and Proctor 2008, 303), which includes flexible, supportive, and responsive features that can be useful for emergent readers through fluent readers as well as for struggling readers of all ages (Larson 2009).

Figure 4.1 Digital Book Evaluation Rubric

	Robust Quality	Adequate Quality	Limited or Weak Quality
Reading Options	Readers have options for reading, listening, viewing, or interacting with the text.	Reader options are limited.	No reader options.
User Friendliness	Guides the reader in interacting with the text through robust prompts for accessing special features.	Limited number of prompts.	No prompts provided.
Content	Information is accurate and presentation is interesting and organized. Illustrations aid in understanding.	Information is accurate, but presentation is uninteresting.	Information and illustrations are inaccurate or unneccesary.
Appropriateness	The text and features are appropriate for the intended audience.	One or two questionable elements that need explanation for readers.	Not appropriate for the intended audience.
Polished Appearance	No errors. Illustrations are positioned near appropriate text.	One or two editing errors that do not interfere with reading.	Numerous editing errors.

(Adapted from Elizabeth Dobler and Daniel Donahoo, Literacy Beat Blog)

eReader Features

Text-to-Speech

Most eReaders have a built-in text-to-speech feature. Text-to-speech, at its most basic level, allows for the reading aloud of a text by a digital device. Is there evidence that it is valuable for a reader to be able to listen to someone reading a text aloud while they are reading? The answer is yes—a number of research studies have found that supporting a reader by offering the opportunity to listen while reading can help to promote reading fluency (Rasinski 1990). There is also evidence that providing a second language learner with a fluently read oral version of the text can help by clarifying pronunciation, clarifying phrase boundaries, and adding the prosodic features that emphasize questions or mood (Brown, Waring, and Donkaewbua 2008). This means that teachers should give serious consideration to giving opportunities to readers, and particularly weaker readers who might be attracted to technology, for encountering texts that offer digitized speech.

It is also the case that synthetic speech is getting better and better, so most text-to-synthetic-speech programs no longer sound robotic and provide good intonation. Some of these programs are quite expensive, but the most sophisticated (such as TextHelp®) will offer instant reading with a pleasant and fluent voice. When a user hovers the cursor over a piece of text—whether it is from an online book, an online newspaper, or a website—that section of text is highlighted, with an additional highlight in a different color as each word is automatically read aloud by the computer.

Various applications of text-to-speech features have been shown to aid young students still learning to read, second-language learners, and readers with dyslexia, language impairments, attention deficits, and visual impairments. The core benefit of text-to-speech is that it lightens the processing load on readers who have difficulty recognizing, seeing, or tracking words in print. Some devices even allow readers to employ synchronized highlighting (a feature that highlights each word or sentence as it is read aloud) and non-speech sounds (e.g., specific alarms that sound to alert a reader to turn the page).

A suite of reading-while-listening opportunities for emergent readers from a variety of language backgrounds comes from the Unite for Literacy group (http://uniteforliteracy.com). Mark Condon began creating these libraries of inexpensive, culturally and linguistically appropriate picture books in the 1990s for students in marginalized communities. This initiative has now blossomed into an online library of dozens of small picture books, with a wonderful bonus: not only can the books be listened to being read aloud in English but there is also a choice of 12 other languages, including Spanish, Chinese, Arabic, French, Russian, and Vietnamese.

Bookmarking and Annotation

Using eReaders allows readers to mark certain sections or pages of text as they read. This feature enhances the capacity for readers to label, annotate, and aggregate their bookmarks with other readers. These tools support reflective and collaborative reading as students use them to demonstrate what they are attending to as they read and later to reflect on what they have annotated during discussions or in writing. Digital annotations can be especially useful for struggling readers who may depend on these sorts of organizational supports to effectively navigate texts. In addition, these tools provide a social context for reading, turning an individual's reading reflections into a collective activity where insights can be shared, compared, and built on collectively and collaboratively. This interactivity with eTexts maximizes the connections between reading, writing, and communicating ideas, each of which is central to college and career readiness and necessary for participation in a digital-information age.

Search Tools

Search tools are also available within eReaders. These tools offer readers the ability to rapidly locate target information or access a search engine to go beyond the text to background material that may enrich their understanding of what they are reading. In this way, students can extend their knowledge and make useful connections to what they are reading. Outside searching also aids students in following their individual interests, a practice that promotes engagement in reading. In the process, students are able to make connections across different texts. Creating space for classmates to share what was learned from their outside reading brings new perspectives to bear in discussions.

Embedded Multimedia Supports

Many eTexts can include multimedia supports, such as links that provide readers access to additional background knowledge or vocabulary supports. Readers can discover the meaning of unfamiliar words quickly and easily without having to shift focus from the text. To enrich the educational content, eText designers and authors are also able to embed additional forms of media within eTexts. Making video elements available within texts makes it possible for students to replay segments. This can be especially useful to those learners who need multiple exposures to dynamic and engaging content to absorb concepts. These features can help teachers respond to the needs of diverse student populations within their classrooms and their varied experiences and background knowledge.

 Common Core to the Fore

Connecting Standards to the Use of eBooks

There are many reasons to incorporate the use of eBooks in your classroom, one of which is the emphasis within the Common Core State Standards to "expose students to a range of print and nonprint texts in media form old and new" (CCSS 2010, 4). Doing so will support "ability to gather, comprehend, evaluate, synthesize, and report on information and ideas to conduct original research in order to answer questions or solve problems." (4).

Using eReaders in Classrooms

In a recent classroom-based cross-cultural study, middle-grade students from Ireland and the United States read eBooks on digital-reading devices (Amazon Kindles™), and participated in literature-circle discussions on an asynchronous blog where they shared responses to text on a message board. These digital experiences allowed them to interact with and respond to the texts they read in new and innovative ways (Dwyer and Larson 2014).

A small group of students, each of two classrooms, was provided with an Amazon Kindle™ loaded with eBook versions of two young adult novels: *The Miraculous Journey of Edward Tulane* by Kate DiCamillo (2006) and John Boyne's *The Boy in the Striped Pajamas* (2006). Students read the books and used the eReader to highlight sections of text and create annotations. Following instruction that provided an overview of the eReader's features, students were observed adjusting the text size, font, and color to suit their personal preferences, accessing the built-in dictionaries, and searching for key words or phrases in the texts. The small groups within each class composed digital thinkmarks on the electronic texts as they read and met face-to-face in a literature-circle format to discuss their responses to and interpretations of the texts. To broaden their discussion and to promote wider dialogue about the texts, each group of students formulated questions and discussion prompts that they posted on the message board blog shared with the other class. These classroom practices supported engaged reading characterized by the development of a reading community that was marked by peer collaboration and high levels of insightful reading response.

Voices from the Classroom

Examining Students' Use of eReaders over Time

Initially, students described in Dwyer and Larson's 2014 examination of eReaders in two middle grade classrooms drew attention to the supports provided by the eReaders. Students shared that, "We really like the vocabulary in these chapters. We used our Kindle™ dictionary to look up words." They were also drawn to the features that allowed them to express individual identity through the use of style signatures and emoticons ("From Katie! xx :)"), font theme and size, color, and highlighting features to draw attention and identify who they were ("Heyyyy its Judith!!"). Over a short period of time, these initial uses of the eReader's features gave way to increased engagement with the texts through the use of highlighting and annotations that contained reflections relating the texts to their own lives. Colm remarked, "It was the same like how Bruno moved from fancy and great to a small and awful house. I used to live in Australia and we had a nice house and a pool and pretty much everything, but when we moved to Ireland, I got stuck in this little house with no pool or anything, and I had to leave all my friends as well <:(."

In another instance, Elizabeth made an annotation that indicated a thoughtful characterization. She shared, "The father is ridiculous and very rude. I can't believe he would treat his family like that. I wonder if they had child abuse services back then. If they do, he should be turned in immediately." eReaders make space for reflection during reading, which promotes such rich insights to be recorded and shared with others.

Pause for Thought

Reflecting on the Use of eReaders to Support Literacy

- In what ways might reading an eBook be the same as reading a traditional bound book? In what ways is it different? Discuss the similarities and differences with your students and invite them to reflect on these comparisons as they use eReaders more frequently.

- How might the opportunity for students to adjust text size, font, and text color on an eReader be distracting for students? How might these preferences be beneficial and/or motivational?

- What eReader features would be beneficial to model for students? Which might be best discovered on their own or pointed out by a peer?

- How would you go about creating an eReading community in your classroom that encourages careful reflection and insightful connections to the text?

eReaders Encourage Interactivity with Texts and Peers

Using eReaders in the classroom shifts the nature of reading activities from an individual activity to one that can be more interactive and social in nature. The social context that the teacher puts in place, in particular, influences how learners make sense of, interpret, and share understandings. This interactivity increases purposeful, text-focused interactions with peers, that in turn can nurture a richer interpretation of text.

Integrating opportunities to share ideas within a community of readers fulfils an important need because many students, especially adolescents, are driven by social interaction. Inviting students to use features, such as marking up the text and adding their own insights as annotations that can be shared with others encourages reading comprehension as a social activity and encourages students to co-construct meaning with their peers.

Implementing collaborative discussion activities such as book clubs, literature circles, cooperative book-discussion groups or idea circles are highly complementary with the use of eReaders. Each of these activity structures provides space for students to dialogue about their annotations and makes room for the discussion of ideas prompted by the text (for ideas about discussion activities see Resources for Book Clubs at http://www.bookbrowse.com/ reading_guides). These open-ended discussion forums create space for multiple interpretations of the text and serve to promote a reliance on textual evidence.

No matter the structure of the reading activity, the purpose is the same—to create a community of readers who construct understandings together. The text mark-up features built into eReaders encourage reflection and promote active participation in discussions. Participation motivates students to read for a range of purposes, use knowledge gained from previous experiences to generate new understandings, and actively engage in meaningful social interactions around reading. Implementing discussion-based classroom routines tangibly illustrates to students that sustained reading has a social purpose and is more than a solitary self-fulfilling activity.

eReaders Encourage Reading as Inquiry

The use of eReaders and the process of adding annotations to text encourages students to ask questions of the text, create connections to classroom activities, and summarize important ideas within the text itself. In addition, they can facilitate a process in which students highlight important ideas in order to share these with peers. In essence, eReaders allow students to have a conversation with the text through the use of annotations. These annotations make students' thinking visible and traceable.

The activities you can implement with eReaders before, during, or after reading can be structured to fit the teaching and learning needs of a given classroom. For example, if you are promoting a focus on summarizing, you can first model this behavior with your class, using a projected article, and then circulate as students work on this strategy themselves. You may then want to layer in a focus on making connections to classroom activities, again modeling how you might do this, then offering students the opportunity to do the same.

One key to turning reading into a process of inquiry is to start with the strategy of posing questions of the text. Posing questions allows students to situate themselves in a position of inquiry as they read and provides a way for them to monitor their own comprehension throughout the reading process. Students can use the annotation feature on an eReader to record these questions. Then, they can share questions with other students in the classroom, which offers the additional benefit of providing time to discuss ideas with others. Implementing discussion structures that encourage students to share their questions in a public forum and space where they can work together to answer the questions can provide a deeper understanding of the text.

Acquiring eReaders for Classroom Use

While eReaders are becoming more affordable than ever before, they are still not standard issue in classrooms. If you are looking to acquire eReaders for use with your students, look to funding sources such as your school-site council, parent teacher association, or Title I resources. In partnership with other teachers from your school, you may even be ready to establish community-school partnerships with local retailers to fund the purchase. Keep in mind that students also may have eReaders at home that they could bring and use on BYOT (bring your own technology) days.

Writing Digital Texts with Your Students

The Internet has transformed the way today's students read, write, and communicate. Readers are no longer consumers who simply appreciate books. They are also producers who actively respond by sharing opinions on what they have read and crafting their own stories in a similar style. The Internet has made it possible for writers to reach a wide audience almost instantaneously. In many classrooms we have visited, writing for an online audience has increased students' motivation to revise and edit their work so that virtual readers can grasp the ideas they want to communicate.

For those teachers who want to create (or have their students create) their own little books, complete with sound files that could embed a reading of the text in any chosen language, Mark Condon's RealeWriter® ("Really Writer") software does the job. Figure 4.2 shows a page from a RealeBook that was created as part of an international book exchange project linking elementary schools in the UK and Texas. The students in the photograph were from a school in England that had created inventions to solve design problems sent by email from a school in Austin. A number of RealeBooks were then published online and also presented to each student in hard-copy form. The book-exchange project ran for five years.

Figure 4.2 Sample RealeBook Page

Printed with Permission from Colin Harrison

Classroom Connection

Designing and Creating Content for eReaders

It is useful to think about eReaders as both a tool
for accessing books and a platform through which
classroom-created self-published books can be accessed.
Classroom-friendly tools for digital publishing are becoming
much more sophisticated. For example, with iBooks Author®
(http://www.apple.com/ibooks-author), it's now easier than ever to
create interactive and visually appealing iBooks® for iPad®.

The Apple®-provided templates feature a variety of page layouts.
You and your students can add your own text and images using
drag-and-drop. Interactive photo galleries, movies, Keynote®
presentations, 3-D objects, and more can also be embedded.
Completed books can be submitted to the iBooks Store™ in a
few simple steps, and before you know it, your students can be
published authors.

Many teachers are now using the iBooks Author® app to create iBooks®.
Some have used the ePub export option using Apple's word processing
program Pages® to create PDFs that can be stored and accessed on
iPads® or Kindles™ using Kindle Reader™ for iPad®.

As you peruse eBooks, you can see how engaging the tools for
creating eReaders can really be! Self-published books showcase
students' and their innovative teachers' efforts to expand reading
and writing connections. The tools and templates for creating
eBooks make it possible for all students to see themselves as
not only engaged readers but also as accomplished writers who
publish and share their work with a wide audience.

Andrea Santilli's seventh grade class authored an eBook titled *Creatures, Plants, and More: A Kid's Guide to Northwest Florida* which shows a written engaging, interactive field guide that includes numerous images of creatures and plants in Northwest Florida. For those interested in visiting Florida or just reading about it, this book will bring you in contact with fascinating interactive photo galleries and videos along with detailed narrative descriptions.

Mr. Smith's fifth graders created *Two Kids and a Desert Town*. These special education students were greatly motivated to write for an authentic audience. The project integrated technology, provided opportunities for collaboration, and gave students the chance to reflect on their learning processes. Having published this book, and knowing that individuals all over the world have downloaded it and read it, these students will forever see themselves as writers! After the success of *Desert Town*, Mr. Smith's students created a second eBook titled *5th Grade: Reflections on Our Year*. This book showcases the growth made by each student across the year. Reflecting on their progress has encouraged them to see themselves as readers and writers.

Teacher Chris Schillig and his students created a spin-off work called *It Was A Dark and Stormy Classroom*. This book is made up of more than 40 of their collaborations and solo stories—an anthology of crime, murder, and clues that proves that detective fiction is alive and well in the 21st Century.

Challenges and Possibilities

eReaders provide increased access to books and are less expensive than traditional textbooks. Despite the promise of eReading technologies, we must also acknowledge that these technologies are but one solution for improving the reading and learning outcomes for students. Digital books, or eBooks, have the potential to let readers interact with texts in amazing ways that can be both motivating and distracting. However, students still need guidance on how to read carefully and critically and manage their focus.

84

Final Thoughts on eReaders and Digital Books

In this chapter, we demonstrated that eReader technologies make digital texts more interactive and malleable. In addition, students have the ability to employ ancillary reading supports such as dictionaries, and offer the ability to highlight and annotate texts and bookmark sections to share and discuss with others. However, it is evident that eReading technologies have limitations and cannot solve every problem in education, and we should not expect them to do so. For example, text quality remains an important issue, one that can serve as either a barrier to or a facilitator of learning. Although eReading technology has the capacity to improve readers' metacognition and self-regulation, interactivity and interconnectivity can introduce new challenges to these important abilities, ones that we are only beginning to understand.

Questions for Reflection

1. In what ways do eReaders extend new potentials for enhancing the reading experience? In what ways could the features within eReaders be distracting?

2. How might eReaders provide support for struggling readers?

3. How can implementing the use of eReaders help create a community of readers in your classroom? What digital possibilities for extended interaction exist?

Strategies for Teaching the Information-Seeking Cycle: The Process of Searching for Information on the Internet

In this chapter, you will learn:

- how reading skills and strategies change when you move from page to screen; and

- the key skills and strategies underpinning the information-seeking cycle.

After reading this chapter, you will know:

- how to support your students as they develop the essential skills and strategies for conducting Internet inquiry in areas such as formulating meaningful questions, generating and revising search terms, investigating search results with a critical eye, and choosing search engines to suit the purpose of the task.

The Internet and other digital technologies for literacy are flattening our world (Friedman 2005) and changing the way we read, write, communicate, and collaborate. In such an online global landscape, we need, first, to be able to access information quickly, effectively, and efficiently, and second, to be capable of assessing the reliability of that information in terms of accuracy, believability, and trustworthiness. Finally, we need to be adept at synthesizing and communicating that information to others. Learning all these skills is no small feat! While "silver-haired Googlers" may seem to struggle finding information online, researchers (such as Bennett, Matton, and Kervin [2008] and the University College London CIBER Group [2008]) are suggesting that our "digital native" student population is struggling in a similar fashion. Yes, they are great at downloading YouTube™ videos. And yes, they spend a lot of time browsing and surfing on the Web (Ito et al. 2010; Rideout,Foehr, and Roberts 2010). But—and it's a big but—when it comes to finding information online and using the Internet as a means to deep learning, problem solving, and developing conceptual knowledge, our students are floundering. Most students go online without a plan of action in mind; they struggle to generate and revise search terms, they click randomly on search results, they quickly become discouraged and lost in an ocean of information, and they rarely engage in any meaningful critique of what they are reading in terms of accuracy, depth, and believability. So, as teachers, we need to support our students in developing the key skills, strategies, and dispositions to successfully use the Internet as a tool for literacy and deep learning.

In this chapter, we will look at the *process* of finding information online. We will focus on the essential skills and strategies for formulating meaningful questions, generating the most efficient search terms, investigating search results with a critical eye, and selecting appropriate search engines for online information searches. In Chapter 6, we will return to the information-seeking cycle to look at the *product* of searching for information online: locating information quickly and efficiently, evaluating and critiquing online information, and synthesizing and communicating that information to others.

Moving from Page to Screen

Before we consider what the information-seeking cycle is, let us reflect on the differences between reading online and reading print-based text. Certainly there are similarities between reading a book and reading text online. These include foundational reading skills, such as rapid decoding and recognition of words and reading fluency, and strategies, such as questioning the text, monitoring understanding, identifying and locating information, and evaluating text (Pressley and Afflerbach 1995). However, online reading introduces additional complexities for the reader as well as higher levels of strategic processing. Further cognitive skills, strategies, and affective dimensions may be required to fully exploit the Internet's potential as a tool for literacy and deep learning (DeSchryver and Spiro 2008).

So, what are the key differences between reading a book and reading online text? Here are some of them.

- **Online text is nonlinear and multimodal.** The print-based reader may choose to read nonfiction or fiction text in a nonlinear fashion, skipping the descriptive passages in a novel to get to the heart of the action, for example. However, the body of printed text is a fixed entity within the confines of the covers of the book. The reader is aware of exactly where they are in a print-based text and the length of such a text. You know when to slow down and linger to savor the dying embers of a novel! In contrast, online text is more fluid, dynamic, and nonlinear by nature. In addition, text is no longer supreme, and information is presented in a composite of multiple modes of representation, such as video, audio files, images, and graphics.

- **Online reading involves active decision-making processes.** Colin Harrison (2011) once noted that the Internet is like a room with 25 billion doors. The online reader chooses which of those doors (hyperlinks or Web pages) to open. So the text, in a sense, is assembled by the active decisions of the reader as he or she finds a pathway to information through a labyrinth of websites and Web pages. Reading in an online environment involves active decision-making and self-regulation processes. It requires a disposition for persistence and resilience when the going gets tough to avoid becoming discouraged or disoriented when presented with what can often be an overwhelming amount of information.

- **Online reading fuses a broad range of prior knowledge sources.** In a print-based text, the reader draws on a range of prior knowledge sources to make sense of the text, such as prior topic and vocabulary knowledge, prior text-structure knowledge, and world knowledge. The online reader draws on similar prior-knowledge sources but needs to supplement these by drawing on prior knowledge of navigational and online-user skills (e.g., being able to activate browser features) and online informational text-structure knowledge (e.g., reading the menu and hyperlink activation). The Internet also introduces the possibility of rapidly updating prior knowledge to new knowledge on-the-hoof as the reader gathers, sifts, and synthesizes information across websites in the malleable moments of Internet searching.

- **The Internet is an open-network environment.** Critical evaluation skills are of paramount importance to assess the accuracy, trustworthiness, and authority of online information. Research suggest that adults (Fogg et al. 2001), adolescents (Leu et al. 2008), and elementary school students (Dwyer 2010), rarely critically evaluate what they read online. Fake or erroneous information posted online may range on a continuum from that of a prankster to a post of a more sinister nature. For example, a report in *The Times* newspaper in the U.K. listed *Masal Bugduv* at number 30 in a list of 50 rising stars in soccer (European football). A number of top premiership clubs, including Arsenal and Liverpool, were reported in the newspaper as being interested in signing the young player. However, *Masal Bugduv* was in fact a nonexistent player whose name was curiously phonetically similar to the title of a story in the Irish language called *M'Asal Beag Dubh*, a story of a pretty useless donkey. A prankster had created the fictitious player by posting snippets of information on blogs and football (soccer) forums over a period of time. The result was red faces at *The Times*! At the other end of the spectrum are hateful websites such as Stormfront, a white-supremacist group that was designed to discredit the life and work of Dr. Martin Luther King Jr. We will look at this particular website in Chapter 6 when we consider how to develop critical evaluation literacy skills for online information.

These changes to reading when we move from page to screen impact how we find information online in what we call the *information-seeking cycle.*

The Online Information-Seeking Cycle

The information-seeking cycle is an exercise in problem solving and involves a complex orchestration of a repertoire of skills, strategies, and dispositions in both reading and information-seeking skills. When we search for information online, we are engaged in a multifaceted, dynamic, opportunistic, and iterative cycle. Figure 5.1 shows the stages within the information-seeking cycle. The stages include goal planning and formulating questions, generating and revising search terms, investigating search results, locating and critically evaluating information, and synthesizing and communicating information to others. Each stage in the cycle is interlinked, and competence at each stage is necessary for the successful completion of the information-seeking cycle.

Figure 5.1. Stages of the Information-Seeking Cycle

For example, an ability to generate effective search terms facilitates the return of a list of relevant search results. The ability to self-regulate in terms of planning, questioning, monitoring, and evaluation is important to monitor online activity. The ability to successfully engage with the *process* of Internet inquiry leads to the location of relevant information for the task focus (i.e., the product of that search). As the Internet is an open-networked system where anyone can publish any information, critical evaluation skills are crucial to ensure success. The reader must also make intertextual links across myriad websites and summarize, synthesize, and transform information into knowledge.

Common Core to the Fore

Online Reading and Writing Within the Common Core State Standards

Reading on the Internet requires additional skills beyond those required during traditional print reading. Many of these higher-order online reading-comprehension skills now appear in the Common Core State Standards. For example, students are expected to: 1) conduct online searches to acquire useful information efficiently; 2) draw information from multiple print or digital sources to locate an answer to a question or solve a problem efficiently; 3) gather relevant information from multiple print and digital sources and assess the credibility and accuracy of each source; 4) use technology, including the Internet, to produce, publish, and interact with others about writing while also recognizing the strengths and limitations of various technological tools; and 5) select and skillfully use digital tools that are suited to meeting specific communication goals.

The key skills and strategies for the *process* stage of the information-seeking cycle are shown in Figure 5.2. Students also need to develop habits of mind and key dispositions, such as self-regulation, self-efficacy, persistence, resilience, intrinsic motivation, and an ability to set learner-centered goals to be successful in the information-seeking cycle.

So, how do we begin to support our students as they develop the key skills and strategies necessary to successfully find information online? A first step is to ascertain the current capabilities of your students when searching for information online. Let's look at what novice third-grade students do when searching for online information.

Figure 5.2 Essential Skills and Strategies within the Information-Seeking Cycle

Information-Seeking Cycle	Key Skills and Strategies
Goal Formation/ Asking Questions	• Asking questions • Planning a strategy • Anticipating challenges • Activating prior knowledge sources
Generating Search Terms	• Generating vocabulary (e.g., synonyms, superordinates) • Monitoring, judging, evaluating, and repairing
Investigating Search Results	• Navigating, interrogating, and negotiating search results • Monitoring and evaluating

 Voices from the Classroom

"There are no rabbits on the Internet"
An illustrative example of what students in a third-grade setting know about searching for online information (Dwyer 2010)

Katie and her classmates Miriam and Nelly were given an Internet information challenge by their teacher: Could they find information on the Internet to help a friend who had a sick rabbit? For the Sick Rabbit task, the students were using Yahooligans™, a search engine designed for students with a facility to search by keyword or browse by category. The students did not discuss the task or plan a strategy for their search. Instead, they launched directly into the task by inputting "rabbit" into the search box. A rather unhelpful error message was generated: "No matches, try again." The students took this message literally and in turn inputted "rabbits," "Rabbit," and "rabbit," to no avail.

Then, they decided to browse by category. The categories included mammals, fish, insects, birds, amphibians, and reptiles. They were unaware that they should search for rabbits under the category of mammals. Miriam wondered if it would be found under insects. Katie thought that maybe they would find rabbits under "amhibions" (sic). Nelly admitted, "I haven't got a clue." The students were distracted by advertisements and images of animals ("Oh, that's so cute!"). When they finally activated a search-result screen, they clicked on the first result displayed rather than skimming and scanning the range of results. After a rather frustrating search, the students retrieved no information related to the task focus. The lack of success in finding any information related to the information challenge led Katie to declare, "You should have rabbits. They do with dogs. But there's just no rabbits on the Internet." Miriam wondered, "Is that the way the Internet works?" Katie retorted, "Yes, that's what the Internet is all about." This led Nelly to conclude, "Well, maybe if the rabbit is sick, the friend should go to the vet."

This classroom illustration exemplifies some of the difficulties experienced by our students when searching for information during the information-seeking cycle on the Internet. You will have noticed that the students engaged in a minimal level of planning and revision of the search terms generated. The students were impulsive in their decision-making processes, adopting a snatch-and-grab approach with minimal scrolling of results. They were hampered by a limited range of vocabulary related to the topic. They were also hindered by the rather poor error message, indexing, and abstraction of hyperlinks on the Yahooligans™ search engine. Their level of frustration, fueled by their lack of success, was palpable.

In the sections that follow, we will discuss effective strategies to help students to conduct the information-seeking cycle effectively, thus enabling them to learn with and through the Internet.

Getting Started with Internet Inquiry

So where to begin? How do you assess the current strengths and needs of your students in conducting the information-seeking cycle? An online information challenge will provide both formative and summative learner-centered assessment (Tierney 2000). You can either physically observe your students conducting an information challenge and make notes, or you can capture a video of online activity, using software programs such as Screencast-O-Matic, Camtasia®, or Jing® for later viewing and analysis (see Appendix B for URLs). Analysis of these information challenges on the key stages of the information-seeking cycle (planning and focusing on task goal, generating and revising search terms, investigating search results, locating information for the task focus, critical evaluation of the information, and summarizing, transforming, and communication of information retrieved) will provide information on (a) the current capabilities, strengths, and needs of students in conducting Internet inquiry within the information-seeking cycle, (b) a starting point for planning a series of mini-lessons involving explicit strategy instruction based on observed needs, and (c) baseline evidence from which to assess students' progress in developing online skills and strategies.

Some examples of these Internet inquiry-information challenges could include:

- How do owls hunt at night without bumping into trees?

- How do Burmese pythons swallow small animals whole?

- What caused the downfall of the Mayan civilization?

In Figure 5.3, we suggest ways to audit what your students already know or can do when searching for information during Internet inquiry.

Figure 5.3 Internet Inquiry Information Challenge Task

20 Minute Timed Quick Task

Choose an Internet inquiry-challenge question from the following choices:

- *How do owls hunt for small animals at night without bumping into trees?*
- *How do Burmese pythons swallow whole animals without choking?*
- *What caused the downfall of the Mayan civilization?*

1. Brainstorm: What do I know about this topic?

_____

_____

_____

_____

_____

2. Which search engine(s) did I use?

_____

_____

3. Which modality did I use? (e.g., text/image/video)

_____

4. Generate search terms: What search terms did I use? Why did I use those search terms?

Search Terms Used	Rationale for Choosing Search Terms

5. Investigate search results: Which search results did I use? What clues did I investigate? Where did the result come on the list of search results? Did I explore beyond the first page of search results?

Clues used				
Where on list of search results?				

6. Critical evaluation of information: How did I evaluate the reliability, accuracy, and currency of the content? What information did I find to answer the inquiry questions? List and be ready to discuss strategies used during post-activity discussion.

_____

_____

_____

Explicit Strategy Instruction: The Gradual Release of Responsibility Model

Once you have identified the current capabilities, strengths, and needs of your students in conducting Internet inquiry within the information-seeking cycle, you can plan a series of mini-lessons to explicitly teach them the specific skills and strategies to conduct Internet inquiry effectively and efficiently. We suggest that you teach students these mini-lessons through the Gradual Release of Responsibility model (Pearson and Gallagher 1983; updated by Duke and Pearson 2002).

In this model, the high degree of teacher support diminishes as students develop competence and assume more responsibility for a learning activity. Figure 5.4 shows how the high level of teacher support diminishes as the students assume control of the strategy.

Figure 5.4 Gradual Release of Responsibility Model

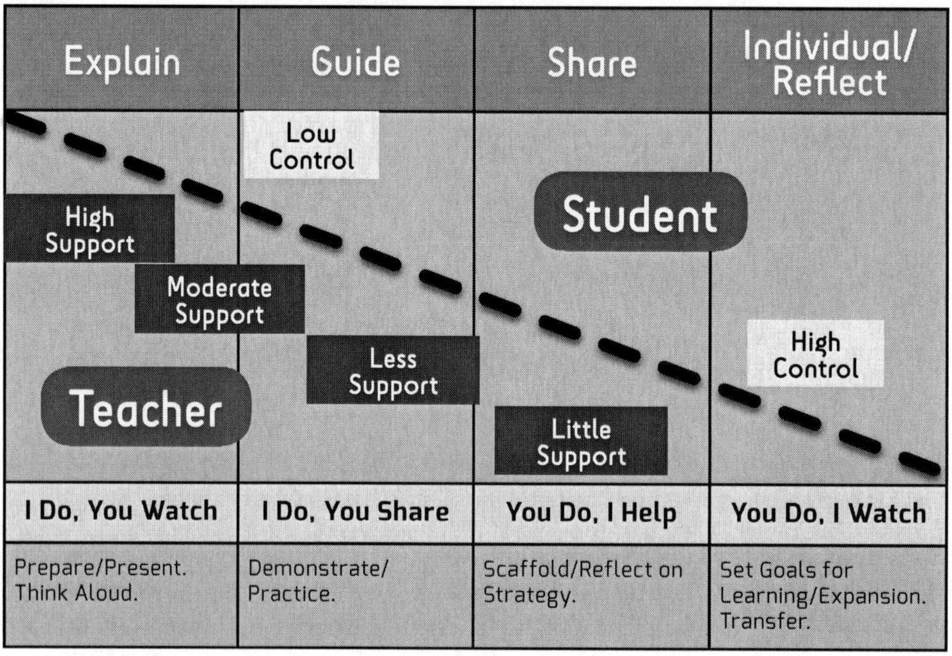

Explain
Guide
Share
Individual/ Reflect
Low Control
Student
High Support
Moderate Support
Less Support
Teacher
Little Support
High Control
I Do, You Watch
I Do, You Share
You Do, I Help
You Do, I Watch
Prepare/Present. Think Aloud.
Demonstrate/ Practice.
Scaffold/Reflect on Strategy.
Set Goals for Learning/Expansion. Transfer.

Adapted from Pearson and Gallagher 1983

In the first stage, the teacher provides explicit instruction of the strategy, naming the strategy and stating why it is an important strategy for the online reader. This is followed by demonstration of the strategy, using think-aloud techniques (Davey 1983), in the form of a mini-lesson in which students observe the teacher as he or she provides explicit examples of (a) what the particular strategy is (declarative knowledge), (b) how to use it (procedural knowledge), and (c) when and why the strategy is used (conditional knowledge). This is the *I do, you watch* stage. Explicit instruction is followed by scaffolding where students help the teacher to apply the particular strategy (*I do, you help* stage) as the teacher gradually releases responsibility for the strategy to the students (*You do, I help* stage). Through guided instruction and peer-to-peer collaboration, students assume autonomous control of the strategy and take responsibility for both activating and monitoring the independent use of a particular skill or strategy as the teacher monitors (*You do, I watch* stage). Peer collaboration assumes greater importance in an online environment as students develop effective online strategies from one another. We will return to the importance of peer collaboration in an online environment in Chapter 7.

Setting a Purpose for Internet Inquiry

The Internet provides easy access to information, and multiple modes of representation of information are available, including video and audio files and graphics. Some have, however, expressed concerns about the superficiality of learning and the depth of conceptual knowledge generated during online reading (Birkerts 1994). Agosto (2002) also has cautioned against what she terms the *consumerist behavior* of students, where students find only sufficient information to satisfy their information needs and do not go deeper. Our challenge as educators is to plan carefully to ensure that our students engage fully with Internet inquiry and develop deep learning and conceptual knowledge online.

For purposeful reading and inquiry on the Internet, it is important for students to formulate engaging questions to provide a purpose for their inquiry, set a context for problem solving, and establish a goal for learning (Owens, Hester, and Teale 2002). Burke (2002) has also noted that when students articulate the goal of an Internet inquiry, they are developing habits of mind by developing a thoughtful and inquiry-based stance.

However, in reality, few of us engage in mapping out a strategy before we launch into an information search. This lack of planning adds to the feeling of frustration we all experience when the expectation is that the answer to a poorly formed question is a mere click away (Kuiper and Volman 2008).

When students develop their own self-generated question for Internet inquiry, their quest for information is more meaningful, as it was derived from their own current topic knowledge and inquisitiveness. In order to support students to develop meaningful questions, you need to do the following:

- **Demonstrate and model different types and kinds of questions** using the Gradual Release of Responsibility model.

- **Develop a metalanguage for questions** so students can discuss and distinguish between literal, *thin* questions requiring one right answer, and higher-order *thicker* questions requiring students to think and search for information across multiple modes of representations and websites.

 ## Voices from the Classroom

Thick and Thin Questions

Vicky, a fifth-grade student, explains, "A thick question is a question that you have to look up; a thin question is a question that's right there. Thick questions [are questions about] something that you're really interested in, instead of stuff that you already know."

- **Build prior domain knowledge of the topic.** For example, in a unit related to animal adaptations to their environments, students initially developed their conceptual knowledge of what the term *adaptations* entailed. This enabled them to draw on this prior knowledge to develop questions to investigate animal adaptations to a particular self-chosen biome.

- **Develop situational interest** through field-trips, science experiments, and expert visits to spark interest, deepen curiosity, and support students in formulating deeper levels of questions on the focus topic.

The online reader should determine a purpose or goal, formulate a flexible plan, and develop resistant strategies to anticipate and overcome barriers to success. The subsequent sections discuss the following strategies related to formulating goals for Internet inquiry:

- KWL (Ogle 1986) and Concept Mapping
- Digging deeper with questions
- Brainstorming and categorizing
- Narrowing a topic

Developing Questions

KWL and Concept Mapping

Strategies for developing questions based on a thematic approach include the KWL strategy. Using this strategy, students could stop-think-talk in small groups to create a three-column chart where they record what they **K**now (or think they know) about a topic, what they **W**ant to know, or what they **W**onder about a topic by generating focus questions, and what they **L**earned following an Internet inquiry. Students need to revisit the **K** section of the graphic organizer to review their initial knowledge and update it in accordance with what they learned. Some questions may not have been answered or new questions may have been generated, and this may lead to further inquiry.

Concept maps are graphical tools for organizing and representing knowledge. They can be used to brainstorm and record graphically the current knowledge of students. Concept maps can be created by using online tools such as Webspiration® (http://www.mywebspiration.com/); apps for education, such as Popplet which was created for the iPad® (http://popplet.com/); or by using currently open source digital tools, such as Bubbl.us (https://bubbl.us/), Cmap tools® (http://cmap.ihmc.us), or Creately™ (http://creately.com/).

Digging Deeper with Questions

You can support your students in digging deeper with questions by presenting mini-lessons focused on the different types and kinds of questions. In addition, we have found that providing students with opportunities to work collaboratively in small groups, to discuss, to brainstorm, to generate and capture ideas, and to reflect and build on the ideas of others helps students to dig deeper with questions (Dwyer 2010). Providing students with a share board where they can showcase questions supports students in monitoring and reflecting on the different types of questions they are formulating to focus Internet inquiry. This forum can be a physical share-board space within the classroom, such as a bulletin board or whiteboard, where students can post their questions and share and alert other class members to the focus questions they are investigating in an online environment. Alternatively, online share boards can also be created by using digital technologies. Digital tools can be used to generate electronic sticky notes, using, for example, Padlet (http://padlet.com), Stormboard (http://stormboard.com), or NoteApp (http://noteapp.com) (see Figure 5.5 for an example). More sophisticated online spaces for sharing, annotating, organizing, and archiving can be created using tools such as Diigo (http://www.diigo.com) or Edmodo (http://www.edmodo.com/home), which allows teachers and their students to safely share ideas in real time to promote social learning in classrooms.

Figure 5.5 Sample Share Board of Questions Created by Fourth-Grade Students Using NoteApp

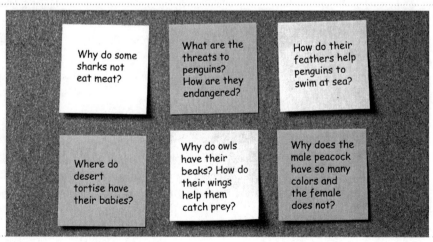

Printed with permission from NoteApp

102

Brainstorming and Categorizing Questions

Using this strategy, students create a list of possible questions to focus their online inquiry. Then, students stop-think-talk to discuss and review the list and see if they can categorize the items into superordinate categories according to the discipline. Figure 5.6 shows how fourth-grade students categorized a list about penguins into conceptual categories related to science, such as diet, appearance, habitat, reproduction, and movement. For example, the students categorized the question *Do penguins feel the cold on their feet?* into the superordinate of *adaptation*; likewise, the question *Do penguins eat anthing eals* [else] *but fish?* was categorized into the superordinate category of *diet*. Students can then decide to focus on one particular superordinate topic related to their chosen subject area or a particular focus question (with many more in reserve for later investigation).

Figure 5.6 Sample Brainstorming and Categorizing Questions into Superordinates by Fourth-Grade Students

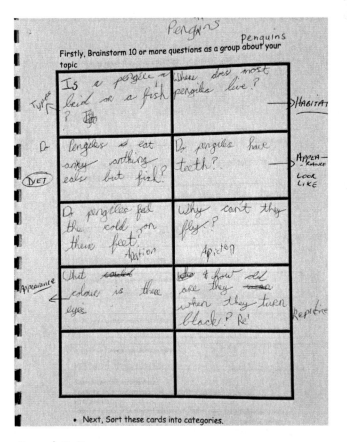

Printed with permission from Bernadette Dwyer

Narrowing the Focus

In the QUEST model, Eagleton and Dobler (2007) suggest using the *Theme, Topic, Focus, Question* strategy for narrowing an Internet inquiry. Using this strategy, students can, for example, narrow the topic from a broad theme to a specific topic and a narrow focus (as shown in Figure 5.7). From this point, students create a question to focus inquiry related to the specific topic and choose the key words from the question.

Figure 5.7 Brainstorming to Narrow the Focus (by Fourth-Grade Students)

Theme	Antarctic animals
Topic	Penguins
Focus	Diet
Question	Do penguins eat anything else but fish?
Keywords	Penguins + diet

(adapted from Eagleton and Dobler 2007)

Choosing a Search Engine

"Let's Google™ *penguin* plus *diet*," suggests Eileen. To *Google*™ has become synonymous with choosing a search engine when seeking information on the Internet. However, there are numerous other search engines and portals that can be used:

1. **Appropriate for elementary students:** askkids™ (http://www.askkids.com), quinturarkids™ (http://quinturakids.com)

2. **More appropriate for older students and those seeking academic information:** Google scholar™ (http://scholar.google.com/)

3. **Directories:** Yahoo™ (http://ie.yahoo.com/?p=us), ipl2 (http://www.ipl.org)

4. **Meta-search engines:** Zuula™ (http://www.zuula.com), Dogpile® (http://www.dogpile.com), Meta Crawler® (http://www.metacrawler.com), Yippy® (http://yippy.com)

5. **Search engines suitable for searching for multimodal representations:** Picsearch™ (http://www.picsearch.com), Truveo® (http://www.truveo.com), Instagrok (http://www.instagrok.com)

Search engines such as Twurdy (http://www.twurdy.com) will also filter results according to levels of readability, indicating texts that are easier or harder to read.

An interesting activity to do with students is to compare and contrast the results for a chosen topic across a number of search engines.

Teachers can support students in choosing an appropriate search engine for the task focus by using functions such as Noodle Tools® or customizing the search engine results using a Customized Google Search™.

Noodle Tools®

Noodle Tools® (see Appendix B for URL) provides a comprehensive guide to a range of search engines to suit particular information needs. By completing a Noodle® quest (see Appendix B for URL), in which you specify parameters for your search, Noodle Tools® will suggest search engines suitable for your task focus. In the screen shot in Figure 5.8, you can see the parameters set for an information quest and suggested search engines suitable for the research topic.

Customized Google Search

Google™ offers a free customized search engine that searches only across sites that are bookmarked by the teacher (see Appendix B for URL). In the screen shot in Figure 5.9, sourced from the Google™ website, Mrs. Gray has bookmarked a series of 17 sites which she has preselected as child-safe sites. They are also chosen because they are highly relevant to the informational needs of her students for the chosen tasks, are reliable sources of information, and match the reading level of the students. This is particularly helpful for the novice online user. It also helps to scaffold and support students' online inquiry processes and makes the time spent online more productive. The number of search results returned is limited, and results are predetermined as being highly relevant to the task focus. One of the advantages of a customized Google™ search is that the focus shifts from the process of Internet searching (locating relevant search results and websites) to the product of that search (the information retrieved for the task).

To locate online information, students must develop effective skills and strategies in both generating and revising search terms and investigating search results with a critical eye. From our own research, we have found a reciprocal facilitation between the ability to generate, criticize, and revise search terms and the subsequent location of relevant information for the online task. This suggests that these overlapping skills need to be developed in tandem. It is also important to develop these skills in the context of authentic classroom activities and projects rather than in decontextualized situations. We turn our attention to generating and revising search terms and investigating search results with a critical eye in the sections that follow.

Figure 5.8 Sample Noodle Tools®: Choosing the Best Search Engine for Your Chosen Task Focus

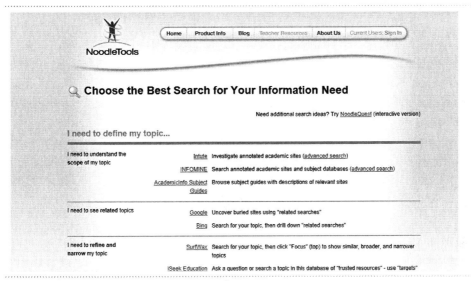

Printed with permission from Noodle Tools®

Figure 5.9 Sample Customized Google™ Search: Example from Mrs. Gray's Research Sites for Kids

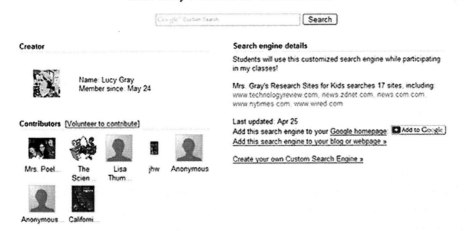

Google and the Google logo are registered trademarks of Google Inc., used with permission.

Strategies to Develop the Generation and Revision of Search Terms

Research suggests that students often struggle to generate and revise search terms to focus online inquiry (Bilal 2000). The difficulties faced by students include insufficient vocabulary knowledge related to the topic at hand, an inability to generate, monitor, and revise search terms, and an inadequate knowledge of how search engines work.

Some key strategies for generating and revising search terms are:

- Evaluating good and bad search terms—the Goldilocks principle
- Creating a list of keywords, using a visual thesaurus
- Generating key words—skimming and scanning the search-result screen

Evaluating Good and Bad Search Terms: The Goldilocks Principle

Providing students with the opportunity to evaluate a given list of inquiry-based questions and the search terms generated to guide online inquiry is a valuable exercise and provides a window of opportunity into their thought processes. Students are given a list of inquiry questions and the search terms that might be used to answer these questions. Through discussion with their peers, students assess and evaluate whether the search terms generated are "too broad" or "just right," hence *The Goldilocks Principle* (adapted from Eagleton and Dobler 2007).

In the example provided in Figure 5.10, students consider the term *birds* too broad because "it will tell you about every single bird," while *birds + diet* is just right as it "will just tell you about there (sic) diet."

Another useful activity is to ask students to critique the search terms used in a simulated online inquiry task. In the following classroom connection, fifth-graders are critiquing the search terms used in a simulated inquiry conducted by "Mary" related to how Burmese pythons swallow whole animals without choking.

Figure 5.10 Evaluating Search Terms: The Goldilocks Principle

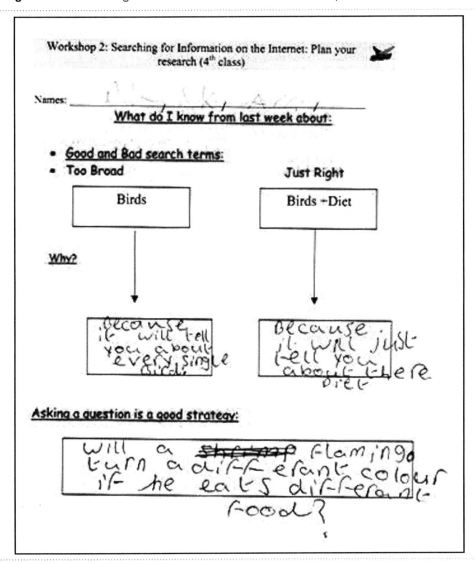

Workshop 2: Searching for Information on the Internet: Plan your research (4ᵗʰ class)

Names: _____

What do I know from last week about:

- **Good and Bad search terms:**
- **Too Broad**   **Just Right**

| Birds | Birds +Diet |

Why?

because it will tell you about every single bird.

because it will just tell you about there Diet

Asking a question is a good strategy:

will a ~~shrimp~~ flamingo turn a different colour if he eats different food?

Printed with permission from Bernadette Dwyer

109

Classroom Connection

Information Challenge: Evaluating Search Terms

Below is a scenario posed to the group of students.

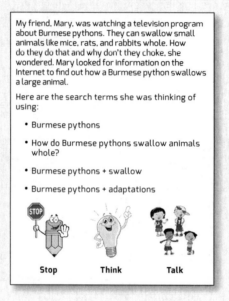

My friend, Mary, was watching a television program about Burmese pythons. They can swallow small animals like mice, rats, and rabbits whole. How do they do that and why don't they choke, she wondered. Mary looked for information on the Internet to find out how a Burmese python swallows a large animal.

Here are the search terms she was thinking of using:

- Burmese pythons
- How do Burmese pythons swallow animals whole?
- Burmese pythons + swallow
- Burmese pythons + adaptations

Stop   **Think**   **Talk**

For the search terms *Burmese python*, the students drew on their prior knowledge of the need to narrow a focus and decided, "It will just tell you about it and not tell you how it swallows it whole." The students deemed *Burmese python + swallow* as "not good because it could come up about birds instead of snakes." Finally, using a question format such as *How does a Burmese python swallow an animal whole?* was judged ineffective by the students as "Questions don't always work on Google." Aileen provided her own helpful search terms for Mary, *Burmese pythons + adaptations + diet*, explaining, "Adaptations like what they eat. I'd pick *diet*, see what they eat, and it would probably tell you what they eat and how they eat it."

Creating a List of Keywords Using a Visual Thesaurus

Students need to be able to create key words in order to generate and revise search terms. This involves generating both synonyms and superordinates for search terms using techniques such as semantic mapping. A number of websites provide access to online generators of words in the form of a visual thesaurus. For example, Snappywords (http://www.snappywords.com), developed by Princeton University, is based on a WordNet® (http://wordnet.princeton.edu) lexical database. Other examples include Visual Thesaurus® (http://www.visualthesaurus.com); and Visuwords.com™ (http://www.visuwords.com).

Generating Key Words: Skimming and Scanning Search Results Screen

Skimming and scanning the search result screen will often provide more useful ideas for generating key words for search terms. The blurb or search result abstract may provide vocabulary that is specific to the subject discipline. Students will require training on how to conduct searches. Search engines like Teoma (http://www.Teoma.com) will suggest associated keywords, alternate spellings, and refined topic suggestions.

Investigating Search Results

Students need to be able to scrutinize and evaluate search results speedily and with a critical eye. Research suggests that students rarely venture beyond the first few results from a returned search results page. They have difficulty unpacking or abstracting the relevance of the search result blurb to the task focus and seldom investigate the search result heading to assess the relevance of the search result to the task (Kuiper and Volman 2008).

Voices from the Classroom

A Cautionary Note

Eileen, a student, shares her concern about using the website summaries to judge the usefulness of a site.

"The blurb might tell you something, but when you go inside, it's something different. Don't get your hopes up if it says what you want to find, 'cause it might not always be inside it."

Students can learn these skills. Analysis from a study conducted by Dwyer (2010) revealed a progression of skills in investigating search results where students moved through three stages:

- A **snatch and grab** random approach, activating the first or second result with minimal reading of search result information.

- A **strategic scrolling** method, systemically investigating each result with some attention given to information provided in the URL or search result blurb.

- A **skillful investigation** procedure, in which the relevance of each result is assessed by critiquing evidence provided by the URL and the abstract paragraph, matching this to the task goal and doing so speedily, efficiently, and automatically.

Students need to develop an investigative questioning stance when evaluating search results by asking questions such as those shown in Figure 5.11. Emulating a detective can help younger students to investigate and scrutinize the clues provided in search results with a more critical eye.

Figure 5.11 Developing a Questioning Stance

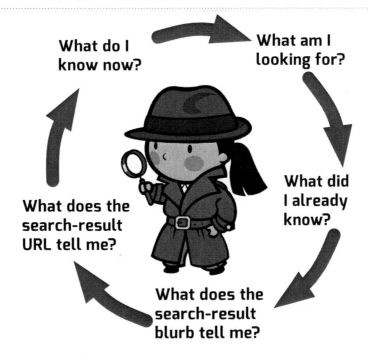

Instructional activities to develop the following strategies for investigating search results will be developed in the sections that follow:

- Investigating the clues provided in the URL

- Scanning the search-result blurb

- Filtering the search results

Investigating the Clues Provided in the URL

A URL (Uniform Resource Locator) is the address of a Web page. Each URL is unique to the Web page that it represents. URLs provide interesting and important information about a website. Figure 5.12 unpacks the elements of the URL (see Appendix B for URL).

Figure 5.12 Unpacking the Elements within a URL

A distributed information system

The message format computers use to exchange information on the Internet. In most cases, it is no longer needed.

Server name. Domain names tell you a lot about the publishers of a website

The subfolder is the name of the file for the page and the subdirectories of where it is stored on the specified computer

http://www.kids.nationalgeographic.com/kids/animals/image.jpg

.com identifies a company or commercial site
.org for non-profit organization sites
.edu for educational sites
.gov for government sites
.net for Internet service providers or other types of networks

If the domain name is two letters, it identifies a country, e.g., **.us** for the United States, **.uk** for the United Kingdom, and **.ie** for Ireland

A structured code for creating websites. Other common extension names include .pdf (portable document format file) using Adobe Acrobat sofware (free to download); .jpeg and .gif, which refer to image files

For example, the domain name prefix, like *national geographic* in *nationalgeographic.com,* will provide information about the publisher of the website. The domain name prefix identifies whether the site is a commercial site (.com), a nonprofit organization (.org), an educational site (.edu), or a website related to a country (e.g., .uk relates to the United Kingdom).

Scanning the Search-Result Blurb

Presenting students with a scavenger hunt of a captured search result is a useful strategy to develop skimming and scanning of search-result URLs and search-result blurbs as students consider the answers to focus questions provided by the teacher. You can capture a search results screen by taking a screenshot of your browser (*Alt + Print* or *Screen* on a PC or Command + Shift +4 for Mac). Give students the search results page and ask them to determine what search terms were used to generate that result. See an example activity in the Classroom Connection that follows, in which students are asked to decide which search result is the most and least useful for the information challenge related to how a Burmese python can swallow an animal whole.

Classroom Connection

Simulated Inquiry for Internet Challenge Activity
How does a Burmese python swallow a small animal without choking?

Brainstorm with a partner (*Think-Pair-Share*) about the following questions and be ready to discuss your choices with the class.

1. Which of the following results would be **most useful** for the Internet question *How does a Burmese python swallow an animal whole without choking?*

2. Which of the following results would be **least useful** for the Internet inquiry question *How does a Burmese python swallow a small animal whole without choking?*

3. What clues are provided in the URL domain name prefix?

4. What clues are provided in the URL domain name suffix?

5. What clues are provided in the search-result blurb?

Burmese Python - wildlife animals, conservation, **adaptation** and ...
www.funzoomiami.org/Animals/Asia/Reptiles/**Burmese-Python** ▾
The **Burmese python** is the largest of the three subspecies of Indian pythons (P. molurus). They have poor eyesight, so they have to rely on specialized receptors ...

Burmese Python: WhoZoo
whozoo.org/students/stamoo/**pythonhtml**.html ▾
Physical description: **Burmese pythons** are one of the six biggest kinds of ... Special anatomical, physiological or behavioral **adaptations**: Pythons are able to ...

Burmese Python Adaptations | eHow
www.ehow.com › Pets ▾
Burmese Python Adaptations. Burmese pythons (python molurus bivitatus) are very large snakes native to Southeast Asia. Females are larger than males and ...

Burmese Python - Animals - National Geographic

Final Thoughts on the Information-Seeking Cycle

The Internet and other digital technologies for literacy present opportunities and challenges as we seek to support students' developing knowledge of the skills and strategies necessary to successfully conduct Internet inquiry. It is clear from this chapter that we need to explicitly teach the skills of goal formation and asking meaningful questions, choosing appropriate search engines for the task focus, generating and revising search terms, and investigating search results with a critical eye. These skills are essential to the process of Internet searching. Students need to develop these skills to a high level so that they can speedily, efficiently, and effectively locate online information. If students spend all of their time online finding a pathway to online information, they will have little left for the product of the information search: locating and evaluating information and synthesizing and communicating it to others. We turn to this topic in Chapter 6.

Questions for Reflection

1. What do you consider to be the main changes when moving from page to screen?

2. How would you assess your students' current capabilities in searching for information online?

3. What are the strategies discussed in the chapter to help students (a) set goals and plan effective questions, (b) develop and revise effective search terms, and (c) investigate search results with a critical eye when searching for information online?

4. What are some challenges and opportunities in using the Internet for literacy and learning in the classroom?

Strategies for Teaching the Information-Seeking Cycle: The Product Stage of Searching for Information on the Internet

In this chapter, you will learn about:

- the components of the *product* stage of the information-seeking cycle: locating, summarizing, transforming, critiquing, and communicating information presented online; and

- the importance of adopting a critical stance to information presented online.

After reading this chapter, you will:

- know how to support your students as they locate online information;

- know how to support your students as they develop critical evaluation skills online; and

- know how to support your students as they develop strategies for transforming, summarizing, synthesizing, and communicating information to others.

In Chapter 5, we reviewed elements related to the *process* of finding online information: formulating meaningful questions, generating and revising search terms, investigating search results with a critical eye, and selecting appropriate search engines for online information searches. Once students have developed skills in these areas, they will have cognitive energy remaining to develop conceptual knowledge of the topic.

In Chapter 6, we return to the information-seeking cycle to consider aspects of the *product* of searching for information online: locating information quickly and efficiently, evaluating and critiquing online information, and synthesizing and communicating that information to others. We will consider each of these aspects in turn in the sections that follow.

Locating Online Information Speedily and Efficiently

Locating information on the Internet is a complex activity. It involves orchestrating a number of skills, strategies, and dispositions for learning. Key skills include locating, transforming, summarizing, synthesizing, and evaluating information. Strategies include skimming and scanning the organizational features of the website, questioning the text (why publish this information?), accessing a wide range of prior knowledge sources (e.g., online informational text-structure knowledge, Internet browser and navigational-skill knowledge, knowledge of the domain topic, and world knowledge). With regard to dispositions, self-regulation (e.g., planning, questioning, and monitoring) and self-efficacy (self-belief, motivation, and engagement) are of central importance to the process. In addition, doggedness, resilience, persistence, and flexibility are crucial to avoid the cognitive overload and disorientation often experienced by online readers.

The key skills and strategies for the product stage of the information-seeking cycle are shown in Figure 6.1.

Figure 6.1 The Key Skills and Strategies for the Product Stage of the Information-Seeking Cycle

Information-Seeking Cycle	Key Skills and Strategies
Locating Information	• Skimming and scanning • Determining important ideas • Classifying information • Comparing information • Activating online informational-text-structure knowledge • Activating navigational-skill knowledge
Critical Evaluation of Information	• Interpreting information • Monitoring and judging relevancy of information • Corroborating and verifying information • Evaluating reliability of information • Making connections to self, to other texts, and to the world • Critiquing information
Communicating Information	• Summarizing information • Synthesizing information • Creating a report • Remixing information • Producing an artifact • Sharing information with others

So, how do we support our students as they locate and read online information? The sections that follow explore aspects of dealing with locating online information: developing online information-text-structure knowledge, utilizing digital tools to support the location of information, and dealing with the information overload to find the needle in the haystack.

Online Informational Text Structure Knowledge

Armbruster and Anderson (1984) reflected on the distinctions between what they termed "considerate" and "inconsiderate" informational texts. Characteristics of considerate texts included the presence of a clear structure (title, introduction, subtitles, tables, typographical layout, and ancillary materials clearly indicated) and coherence (the idea of a text "sticking together" and flowing) at both a sentence and at a whole-text level. Their subsequent attempt at producing an ideal example of a considerate-informational text led them to conclude that "easy reading is hard writing."

Much of the information presented on the Internet is in the form of informational text. Although print-based informational text has similar structures (e.g., headings and subheadings), a number of key differences are important to consider.

Considerate-digital texts on websites provide supports such as organizational cues, presentation cues, support cues, and evaluation/relevancy cues (Eagleton 2005).

- **Organizational Cues:** menu, hyperlinks, icons (e.g., home button), navigational buttons

- **Presentation Cues:** text, images, graphs, maps, multimedia components (e.g., video and audio)

- **Support Cues:** glossary, audio, video links, text-to-speech functionality, FAQs, translations, and search tools

- **Evaluation/Relevancy Cues:** author, organization, stated domain name prefix and suffix, date updated

The following activities can help students develop their knowledge of both online informational-text structure and their navigational skills:

1. Students can compare and contrast print-based information text structures (table of contents, glossary, subheadings, bold/italicized words, graphics, and illustrations) with their website equivalents (menu, hyperlinked glossary, bold/italicized words indicating hyperlinks, navigational aids, buttons, audio, and image supports).

2. Website scavenger hunts help students develop both navigational and information-seeking skills. Scavenger hunts can be based around different levels of simple quiz-type questions, or they can be based around more complex questions (e.g., *When did life begin on Earth?*). They can be teacher-developed within the context of authentic classroom Internet-inquiry projects. Remember to use questions

that focus on lower- and higher-order thinking skills, that activate the content hidden beneath hyperlinks, that help students to build skimming and scanning skills on Web pages, and that facilitate the development of navigational skills by requiring students to move between the home pages and linked pages on websites to find answers to the questions posed. The ReadWriteThink website provides an example of a scavenger hunt on the "Comprehending Nonfiction Text on the Web" lesson plan. Students are asked to find the answers to lower- and higher-order questions based around the Missouri Botanical Gardens/Evergreen Project (See Appendix B for URL).

Supports Offered by Browsers and Search Engines and Digital Tools

Almost all browsers permit viewing adjustments, giving the reader some measure of control over their viewing options. For example, Google Chrome™ allows for a full-page zoom and high-contrast color option. Firefox® offers a readability add-on that de-clutters a website, stripping away irrelevant material such as advertisements. The add-on also allows the reader to customize for viewing preferences (e.g., font size). The Firefox® N-Abled Web Accessibility Toolbar includes options, such as color preference, zoom features, and screen-reader capability.

Speech-enabled Web browser tools add voice to support readers to access online content, thereby supporting students with learning difficulties, students with mild visual impairment, and English language learners. For example, BrowseAloud (http://www.browsealoud.com) is a free digital tool that works with all of the major browsers.

In searching for information, we often give primacy to print-based text. However, the Internet affords us multiple pathways to information through text, image, video, and audio. Helen, a middle school student, was conducting an information challenge related to the downfall of the Mayan civilization (for more on conducting online information challenges, see Chapter 5). She conducted a key-word search and viewed videos related to the topic, then images, and finally text. She explained her strategy: "I usually search for information by looking at videos and images to get the main concepts related to a topic. Then, I will look up some articles when I have this background information."

We explored a range of search engines in Chapter 5. However, in the context of locating information through multiple modes and modalities, the search engine Instagrok (http://www.instagrok.com) merits attention. To *grok*, the developers tell us, is to "understand thoroughly and intuitively." Instagrok presents a visual graph of the key concepts related to a topic. In addition, on the right-hand side of the screen, you can view key facts related to the topic, websites, videos, images, and quiz questions related to the topic. There is also a slide bar at the top of the screen to adjust the level of difficulty of the information presented. You can pin any of these representations onto the visual graph. Figure 6.2 illustrates a grok related to the collapse of the Mayan civilization. What really excites us about Instagrok is that as you conduct a grok, a journal is automatically created showing all of the websites visited, images and videos explored, etc. These journals (See Figure 6.3) are valuable assessment tools for teachers and provide insights into the work of students as they conduct information searches.

Figure 6.2 Sample Instagrok Search Engine Interface

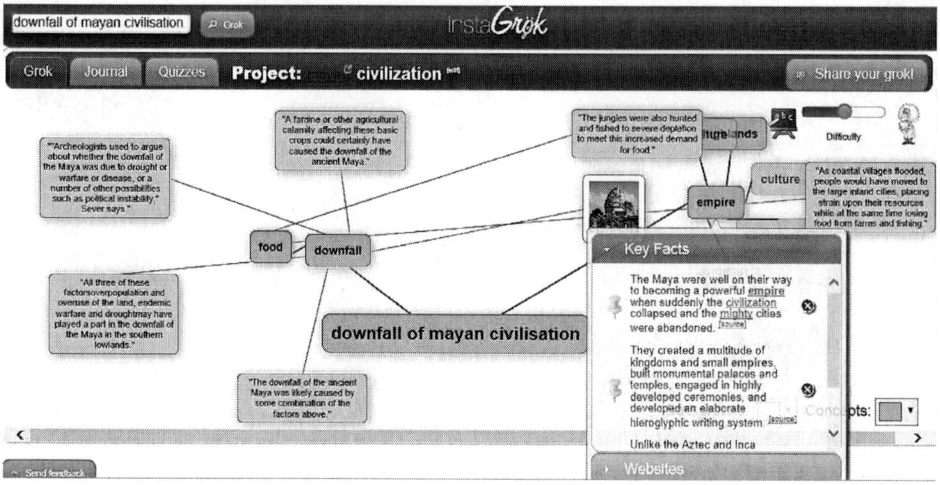

Printed with permission from Instagrok

Figure 6.3 Sample Journal Created Using Instagrok Search Engine

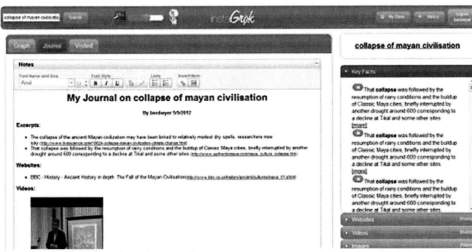

Printed with permission from Instagrok

Students can become frustrated by the readability levels on some websites. Readability levels (e.g., Flesch Reading Ease, Flesch-Kincaid grade level; Gunning fog index; Dale-Chall Formula; Frye readability scale) on websites can be calculated through the use of online tools such as Readability Plus (http://www.micropowerandlight.com/rd.html). Readability algorithms have many limitations and provide only a rough guide to the difficulty of content on websites. A simple strategy for assessing text difficulty on websites for elementary students is the five-finger test. Students raise a finger for every unknown word shown on the screen, and if they raise five fingers while reading onscreen information, the text may be too difficult for them to read at present, a simple but effective strategy!

From Searching for to Locating Information: Finding the Needle in the Haystack

There is so much information available online, and it is often difficult to retrieve the information for a task or a search focus, or "find the needle in the haystack." While *<edit find>* or *<Ctrl Find>* can be useful to quickly highlight a single target word on a webpage, it is less efficient at finding multiple search terms, key phrases, relevant paragraphs, or sections relevant for a search inquiry. There are digital tools available to help you move, as the developers say, "from search to find."

Yolink® (http://www.yolink.com) is an add-on browser-extension tool that scans Web pages, search-engine results, and digitized books to find your inputted search terms and deliver information that is relevant to your inquiry. Yolink® is a supportive digital tool in two ways. First, it enables the reader to dig deeper behind the links without laboriously navigating to and opening each website link in turn. It does this by previewing and filtering the search results and highlighting snippets of information from relevant sections of search results for the reader. Secondly, Yolink® can also search within bodies of texts (e.g., digitized versions of books) for keywords or phrases to find information relevant for a particular research focus.

Bookmarking relevant sites by adding them to your "Favorites" tab is one way to collect and retrieve websites that you visit. Creating subfolders with meaningful names is helpful when you want to revisit a particular website. However, if, like us, you engage in squirreling behaviors in which you tab multiple websites on an hourly/daily basis, you can end up with hundreds of websites in multiple subfolders. Just why you wanted to bookmark a particular website can be lost in the moment of tabbing. It is also difficult to backtrack quickly to a specific website when you want to locate information. So, the proverbial haystack looms again! A digital tool which we have found to be effective for organizing research online is Diigo® (Digest of Internet Information, Groups, and Other Stuff) (http://www.diigo.com). Diigo® is a cloud-based information management tool that enables users to collect, highlight, bookmark, clip, share, and annotate websites. Teachers can create an educator account with Diigo®. This will enable you to generate student accounts and establish collaborative research groups within your classroom. Diigo® is helpful when conducting research, creating personal learning environments, and collaborating with others. Some of the features of this tool that we have found to be useful include:

- Annotating and highlighting snippets of information on websites with sticky notes.

- Saving a screenshot of a website on a particular day to archive the website and revisit to review changes over time.

- Categorizing relevant information through the use of tags and lists on websites for quick retrieval of information.

- Creating collaborative groups in which teams of students can research information and post their findings and annotations for others in the group to review. Members can then interpret, critique, and synthesize information from a variety of online sources.

- Accessing your own digital library, as part of a personal-learning environment, from any computer or through apps on tablets or smart phones.

- Developing professional learning opportunities for teachers through Diigo®-created educator groups.

Summary Checklist for Reading and Locating Information on a Website

Let's take a moment to summarize the key skills and strategies for locating information online that we have covered so far in the chapter.

- Develop online informational text-structure knowledge, such as organizational, presentation, support, and evaluation/relevancy cues.

- Build navigational skills through the use of web-based scavenger hunts.

- Use browser adjustment features, such as font size, zoom features, and speech enabled tools to increase accessibility to content on websites.

- Judge the readability of online content through online-digital tools or the five-finger test of readability.

- Remember that content can be presented in multiple formats and modalities that include text, images, tables, graphics, video, and audio.

- Skim and scan websites to locate relevant information for subsequent close reading. This optimizes the time spent online. Utilize digital tools that enable the reader to locate information speedily and efficiently.

- Bookmark and organize websites visited through highlighting, annotating, and tagging online content. Utilize digital tools that enable readers to research, organize, archive, share, and collaborate with others when researching information.

Evaluating and Critiquing Online Information

The Internet is a largely unvetted open-access media and is available to any individual to publish any information (Leu 1997). In contrast, print-based media, with a five-century-plus start on online media, has a number of traditional mediators and gatekeepers, such as editors, critics, and peer-review processes in place. The Internet has shifted the burden for quality control and assessment of information in terms of accuracy, objectivity, credibility, and trustworthiness onto the online reader (Metzger 2007). Research suggests that the online reader is struggling with the task. For example, in a study involving 2,440 adult participants, found that site presentation in terms of visual design and graphics, was the primary factor in judging the reliability of information on a website (Fogg et al. 2001). In a study conducted by Leu et al. (2008) adolescent students were asked to evaluate the reliability of the spoof website Save the Pacific Northwest Trees Octopus (see Appendix B for URL). Despite indicating in a prior interview that one should not trust online information, 87.5 percent of the students indicated that they thought this site was reliable. When the researchers indicated that the site was indeed bogus, the students persisted in their belief that the site was reliable, citing the updated copyright date and links to the author in their reasoning. In general, the online reader is unwilling to expend much cognitive energy on the task of critical evaluation of online information. In the following section, we will explore the difficulties experienced by students when reading information on websites. It is important to note that critical evaluation is not limited to websites and that one should also check the veracity of information presented on blogs, social networking sites, Twitter® feeds, wikis, etc.

Research suggests that students experience difficulties in realizing that incorrect, false, or misleading information can be posted on the Web (Schacter, Chung, and Dorr 1998); do not challenge the authority and reliability of information presented (Lorenzon 2002); equate the amount of information presented with the quality of that information (Agosto 2002); are often misled by the appearance of a website (Sutherland-Smith 2002); and lack prior knowledge to assess the veracity of information presented and detect hidden author agendas (Burke 2002). An additional complexity in evaluating online information may relate to students' abilities to draw on limited prior experience and world knowledge to assess and evaluate online information.

Students rarely ask important questions as they review online information, such as:

- Is the information trustworthy? Can I depend on it? How can I judge reliability?

- Is the information accurate? Is it believable? How can I tell?

- Do I understand it?

- Does the information satisfy my information needs?

- What is the author's agenda?

Critical evaluation of online information involves an orchestration of a repertoire of skills strategies and dispositions, such as assessing accuracy, credibility, believability, trustworthiness, bias, reasonableness, coverage, relevancy, currency, and readability. Critical evaluation is also dependent on reader motivation and the situational context.

Critical evaluation of online information encompasses:

- **Critical thinking skills**—a disposition for interrogating the text; evaluating arguments, and questioning content

- **Critical reading skills**—an ability to evaluate relevancy, accuracy, and reliability

- **Critical multimedia information literacy skills**—a capacity to critically consume information and to separate the medium from the message

- **Critical literacy skills**—an aptitude to view information as value laden and not neutral

Using the gradual release of responsibility model (Pearson and Gallagher 1983), we can guide our students to evaluate websites by using four strategies:

- Scan Perimeter for Authority

- Dig Deeper for Accuracy

- Scrutinize the Support

- Raise Your Antennae for Details

Figure 6.4 lists questions for evaluating and thinking critically about website information in all four categories.

Figure 6.4 Questions for Thinking Critically about Website Information

Scan the Perimeter for Authority
- Is the author clearly identified on the Web page?
- Do I know anything about the level of expertise of the author?
- Does the author list his or her credentials and years of experience?
- Does he or she provide a link to a résumé or a personal home page?
- Is contact information provided (e.g., email, contact)?
- Is there an identified author of the website or page? Is this site sponsored by an organization?

Dig Deeper for Accuracy
- Are there any references listed as sources of information?
- Is the information consistent with what I already know about the topic?
- Are there any clues on the page to tell me that the information is true?
- Does the author have a particular point of view, e.g., religious, political, etc.?

Raise your Antennae for Details of Reliability
- Is the site based on verifiable facts and opinions?
- Is the topic controversial?
- Did I look at the language used? Did I look for use of personal attacks, use of ridicule, or use of emotive, provocative, or inflammatory language?
- Is the site sponsored by a commercial organization? Is the viewpoint expressed in support of a particular commercial product or a particular political, religious, or social opinion organization?
- Is the argument presented plausible? Does the information appear reasonable?

Scrutinize the Support
- Is the site easy to navigate? Are icons such as home and back buttons clearly indicated?
- Is the website free of spelling or grammatical errors?
- Are there advertisements on the page? Are they clearly distinguishable from the content of the page?
- What are the multimodal components of the site (e.g., video, audio, graphical elements)? Is there a specific purpose for their inclusion?

A sample lesson follows in which the teacher is demonstrating through modeling and think-aloud techniques how to evaluate online information using questions in the four categories. This lesson is suited only for older students, as the content is very heavy. It may be adapted to suit the needs of your classroom.

 # Voices from the Classroom

Evaluating Information on a Website

In this think-aloud, the teacher models and demonstrates how to evaluate a website using the Gradual Release of Responsibility model.

Anyone can publish any information on the Internet. It is therefore important to have your antennae raised to judge the credibility, accuracy, reliability, and sources of the information you read online. So how we do this? We can ask evaluation questions in the following categories:

- Scan the Perimeter for Authority
- Dig Deeper for Accuracy
- Raise Your Antennae for Details of Reliability
- Scrutinize the Support

Let's look at the website about Dr. Martin Luther King Jr. I'm adopting an Inspector Clue-Search stance.

First, I am **scanning the perimeter for authority** *and asking questions. While scanning the perimeter, I see that the URL domain name suffix is a dot-org site, so that's good. I often visit dot-org sites, and they are mostly reliable, but you always need to check further. I'm scanning around the perimeter of the website and notice that the author of this site is not clearly identified, but the site is hosted by Stormfront, and there is a discussion forum.*

Last night, I searched for information on Stormfront and looked at the forum discussion. I now know that Stormfront is a white-supremacist group. This raises a red flag of concern for me.

Now I am asking questions to **dig deeper for accuracy**. I'm beginning to think I need to dig deeper on this website. I start to read some of the information and am thinking this information is not consistent with what I already know about Dr. Martin Luther King Jr. (teacher brainstorms with students what they know about Dr. Martin Luther King Jr). I'm going to look past the first page of the website. One Web page relates to Jews and civil rights. There is no information on the site about this author. Let's see if we can find information or articles about this person (teacher demonstrates searching for information for the author). I can see that this person holds strong views on race and religion. This raises a second red flag for me.

Next, I am **raising my antennae for details of reliability**. I'm scanning the language used on the website. It strikes me that the language is crude, provocative, and insensitive. The site also makes personal attacks on Dr. Martin Luther King Jr. The facts presented do not coincide with what I already know about this person. This raises a third red flag.

Finally, I am **scrutinizing the support** on the website. It's easy to navigate around this site, although some of the links are broken. For example, the links to other pages and the link to the video are not available. Broken links indicate that the website is not being updated very often. Again, a red flag.

I'm skeptical about the information presented on this website even though it is a dot-org site. First, the website is presented by Stormfront, a white supremacist group. Second, the information presented does not coincide with what I already know about Dr. Martin Luther King Jr. The authors cited are not reliable. Finally, the website has some broken links. I'm thinking I should check the information on another website.

I'm going to check some of the information on this site with another site related to Dr. Martin Luther King Jr. (http://www.thekingcenter.org). Can you help me? Scan the perimeter of this website for authority, dig deeper for accuracy, raise your antennae for details of reliability, and scrutinize the support on the website. Use the same questions I used to think critically about the information (teacher can provide students with a copy of the questions in Figure 6.4). Think-Pair-Share with your partner. Be ready to share your findings with the rest of the group. Do you think the information on this site is very reliable, somewhat reliable, or not at all reliable?

Further Online Resources for Developing Critical Evaluation Skills

There are numerous resources online to help students develop critical evaluation skills. Here are some of our favorites (see Appendix B for URLs):

- *The Good, the Bad, and the Ugly,* or *Why It's a Good Idea to Evaluate Web Sources,* authored by Susan Beck, New Mexico State University

- Kathy Schrock's *Guide for Educators*

- 21st Century Information Fluency Project

- Internet Detective

- Criteria for evaluation of Internet Information Resources (authored by Alastair Smith, Department of Library and Information Studies Victoria University of Wellington, New Zealand)

- RADCAB rubric for evaluating online information

- Search the Web and Evaluate Web Resources (University of Maryland University College)

Summarizing, Synthesizing, Transforming, and Communicating Information

Another step in the information-seeking cycle relates to summarizing and synthesizing the information retrieved during Internet inquiry. The information-seeking cycle concludes with the transformation and communication of that information.

Summarization of text often poses difficulties for students, and we know from the research literature that it is developmental by nature, with clear distinctions between older and younger students (Dole et al. 1991). Summarization can involve organizing, sifting, determining, generating, condensing, constructing, and transforming information to capture concisely the essence of a text (Block and Pressley 2002). Synthesizing information involves interpretation, analysis, and evaluation of the summary, where a student re-forms the summary and connects it with his or her own ideas, experiences, and thoughts to create a synthesis of new insights and knowledge. Clearly, difficulties with summarization and synthesis are compounded in an online environment as students deal with an information overload across multiple websites during a search for information. In the sections that follow, we consider how digital tools can aid summarization and synthesis of information.

Summarizing and Synthesizing Information Using Graphic Organizers

Teachers are familiar with the use of graphic organizers for summarization and synthesis. For example, graphic organizers are often used to enable students to recall information, determine importance in text, and represent conceptual knowledge. Graphic organizers should be used judiciously in the classroom. They should be seen as temporary scaffolds to aid students as they develop summarization and synthesis skills and should not become formulaic, workbook-type "filler" activities. Strategies developed using print-based graphic organizers can transfer when using digitized formats of graphic organizers in an online environment. However, one of the advantages of a digitized format of a graphic organizer is flexibility. The graphic organizers explored in the section show how digitized formats of graphic organizers can grow organically and be customized and expanded through student usage. We recommend that students collaborate in pairs or small groups when using these tools. Teachers should model and demonstrate the use of these tools through the gradual release of responsibility model (Pearson and Gallagher 1983).

- Thinking tools and visual-mapping techniques to aid summarization and synthesis can be developed using digital tools. For example, the subscription-based *Inspiration*® (http://www.inspiration.com) and for younger K-5 elementary school students, Kidspiration® (http://www.inspiration.com) software packages allow students and teachers to create graphic organizers. Both are available for free trial periods. With *Inspiration*®, for example, students can access an integrated dictionary and thesaurus, include video and audio components, add hyperlinks to websites, present work in diagrammatic and outline view (with topics and subtopics), and easily share work with others through easy export options.

- *Exploratree* (http://ww.exploratree.org.uk) is a free Web resource with access to a library of interactive thinking and diagrammatic guides. It was developed as part of the Enquiring Minds project (funded by Microsoft). Some of the features include an ability to create your own thinking guide from scratch by adding or changing text, images, shapes, etc. In addition, students can collaborate to create, present, and submit a thinking guide for class projects. For work in the classroom, teachers can choose to reveal thinking guides in stages to encourage class discussions. They can also lock down certain features, such as instructions and hints, on these graphic organizers. These thinking guides can also be printed (up to A0 size).

- There are a number of apps for tablet devices and smartphones that can be used for notetaking to develop summarization and synthesis in the classroom. *DocAS* is an app that permits students to make comments on text as they read. *DocAS* promotes active reading as the student annotates the text with questions, connections, highlights of important information, and summaries of text. *DocAS Lite* is free at the iTunes store; the full version is available for purchase. *Paperport* (currently free) allows you to mark up and annotate a range of documents including pdf files. It differs from *DocAS* as it allows more editing on, for example, a pdf document and includes an ability to add blank or graph pages as well as clipboard contents. Both apps permit audio input and a capacity to import and export from a range of online sources, including cloud-storage devices such as Dropbox or Box.net.

- The ReadWriteThink website (http://www.readwritethink.org), developed by the International Reading Association (http://www.reading.org), has a range of lesson plans to support summarization and synthesis. There are a series of lessons based on the guided comprehension model (McLaughlin and Allen 2002) using a range of graphic organizers to support monitoring, summarization, anticipating difficulties in text, and activating prior knowledge.

 Common Core to the Fore

Communicating Online Information

The CCSS for writing require that students write explanatory texts that introduce and establish a topic and develop that topic using well-chosen, relevant facts, data, details, quotations, examples, or other information. Inherent in the Common Core State Standards is the push to help students develop the ability to interpret and communicate information visually through the use of images, photos, graphs, or figures.

Final Thoughts on the *Product* Stage of the Information-Seeking Cycle

Another step in the information-seeking cycle relates to summarizing and synthesizing the information retrieved during Internet inquiry. In this chapter, we explored a range of skills and strategies to locate, annotate, and summarize online information using a variety of digital tools and apps. In addition, we discussed the importance of developing a questioning and critical stance towards information presented online and investigated a number of strategies for evaluating the veracity, reliability, and trustworthiness of online information. In Chapter 7, we will discuss how collaborative Internet projects promote the exchange of information beyond the confines of the walls of the classroom. In Chapter 8, we will share a range of digital tools that promote the transformation, exchange, and communication of information in a networked world.

Questions for Reflection

1. What strategies were discussed in the chapter to help students locate, summarize, transform, and communicate information found on the Internet?

2. How can the range of multimedia supports offered by a range of browsers and search engines, as explored in the chapter, support the diverse needs of students in the classroom?

3. How can we, as classroom teachers, help our students acquire the skills and necessary strategies to develop critical-thinking, critical-reading, critical-multimedia-information, and critical-literacy skills when reading information on an online platform?

CHAPTER 7

Strategies for Encouraging Peer Collaboration and Cooperative Learning

In this chapter, you will learn:

- why peer-to-peer collaboration is important for the development of key skills and strategies needed to read, write, and communicate online;

- how to create a classroom culture to promote the exchange of Internet reading, writing, and communication strategies among your students;

- how to build productive peer collaboration through the use of online reciprocal roles; and

- a range of online literacy activities that encourage student-to-student collaboration.

After reading this chapter, you will be able to:

- use the reciprocal roles of Questioner, Navigator, and Summarizer to promote effective inquiry-based learning online;

- apply specific instructional strategies and activities to develop the quality of interactions in groups;

- structure literacy experiences that promote quality collaboration among students within and beyond the classroom; and

- incorporate collaborative literacy activities such as Internet projects, email exchanges, and teacher-designed online writing projects into your instructional program.

Voices from the Classroom

Peer collaboration

Vicky, a fifth-grade student, comments on her experiences with peer collaboration: "Three heads are better than one. If you were searching for something, and you are on your own, you don't know how to do it. If you're working in a group, someone else might know how to do it, so they can help you."

New definitions of literacy in the 21st Century position reading as *more* than a set of skills and strategies (Lankshear and Knobel 2001) and literacy education as *more* than a means of promoting academic achievement. The RAND Reading Study Group (2002) drew attention to the importance of reading comprehension and asserted that the text, the activity, and the reader are all situated within a larger sociocultural context. As we work toward creating a community of learners, the culture of the classroom shapes the context and in turn influences how learners make sense of, interpret, and share understandings. The ability to work collaboratively, develop understandings based on multiple points of view, and co-construct ideas with others is highly valued in education and in the workplace.

Over a period of years, Daniels (2002), Raphael, Florio-Ruane, and George (2001), and others have guided teachers' implementation of collaborative reading activities such as book clubs, literature circles, and cooperative book-discussion groups. Whatever the structure these reading activities take in an individual classroom, the purpose is the same—to create a community of learners who co-construct meaning together. It has been our experience that collaboration in its broadest sense is about teamwork—sharing and exchanging ideas with learners who have common goals. This sort of teamwork is vitally important to the contexts that define the 21st Century and can be a useful organizing structure when designing online literacy activities that involve the Internet and new technologies.

Structuring collaborative activities in classrooms can be challenging. For example, some students lack experience in working together toward a common goal and thus find it difficult to share ideas and build on one another's thinking. For these reasons, it is important to create a culture that supports productive collaboration and to teach students the skills required for working together collaboratively. Before we introduce activities that support the development of quality of interactions between group members, we will briefly overview the literature on peer collaboration and cooperative learning.

Peer Collaboration and Cooperative Learning

Johnson and Johnson (1999) suggest incorporating five elements across instructional experiences: 1) positive interdependence; 2) individual accountability; 3) face-to-face promotive interaction; 4) social skills; and 5) group processing. Positive interdependence develops through providing mutual learning and shared goals where success is not achieved at an individual level but rather is shared among group members. With individual accountability, individual group members are responsible for their efforts (or lack of) to the other members of the group. Face-to-face promotive interactions extend and expand learning within a group by, for example, introducing new problem-solving strategies to other group members. Because positive social skills are not inherent but instead learned, group members need to be explicitly taught how to develop interpersonal traits, such as leadership and conflict-management skills. Group processing refers to an ability to act in a helpful, productive manner and to work effectively to identify solutions to problems.

When students collaborate in constructing meaning from text, they have what Kucan and Beck (1997) have referred to as "multiple resources at the reading construction site." Readers can draw on not only their own knowledge and the knowledge of others within the group but also the processes through which that knowledge is constructed (Putney et al. 2000). Constructing meaning through discourse in social settings could later transfer to an internalization of the strategic processes and independent application of strategies by individuals.

Successful collaborative groups engage in "huddling" (Barron 2003), in which group members provide and receive explanations from peers and then challenge them through exchanges that recognize alternative points of view. In the process, groups examine their own knowledge and beliefs, justify opinions, develop a sense of agency in order to problem-solve, pool collective prior knowledge, and build consensus.

However, the literature also cautions about the difficulties of working in groups. These difficulties include surface and basic levels of interaction, the persistent dominance of one group member in directing and controlling activities, and what Kerr and Bruun (1983) have referred to as "free-rider effects," in which individuals adopted a passive and less-engaged role within the group. Free-rider effects can be alleviated by holding group members accountable for their actions to the group, which can help them stay on task within group activities. As will be discussed later in this chapter, roles performed within the group can be evaluated through group discussions and peer- and self-assessment, such as *rate my role*, in which group members review their own and peer performance within the group.

We conducted research (Castek 2008; Dwyer 2010) that explored the development of online literacies with third- through sixth-grade students in Ireland and the United States. In both studies, the online instruction of skills and strategies were initially developed by the classroom teacher, drawing on Pearson and Gallagher's (1983) Gradual Release of Responsibility model. However, scaffolding soon diminished as the students developed online skills and shared them with one another. Results from both studies suggest that the positioning of the teacher changed from a director of learning to that of a co-learner and a facilitator of online learning within a classroom community of learners.

Castek (2008) found that encouraging students to take on leadership roles in sharing their online skills and strategies was a beneficial means of promoting online reading comprehension. Findings from this study suggest that students learn online reading comprehension skills best from other students within the context of challenging activities designed by the teacher. Increased levels of challenge and peer collaboration prompted students to develop novel approaches for making sense of complex information and encouraged them to think deeply about solving problems that involved skilled use of the Internet.

Findings from the Dwyer (2010) study revealed that peer collaboration supported students to actively engage with text and facilitated a deeper processing of text as group members expanded their own individual understanding of skills and strategies through examining, contesting, evaluating, and negotiating with other group members during Internet inquiry. Peer-to-peer collaboration also enabled the groups to apply and hone the skills and strategies developed during explicit strategy instruction and guided practice. As the longitudinal study progressed, social learning seemed to assume greater significance in applying and developing online reading skills and strategies.

In sum, these studies reveal that peer collaboration in an online environment is a vital component in the development of a repertoire of online skills and strategies. There are a number of reasons to provide students with multiple opportunities to discuss and exchange online skills and strategies:

1. **Peers scaffold learning** by sharing and exchanging skills and strategies.

2. **Peers challenge one another's** thinking. Through dialogue within groups, ideas are expanded, contested, and affirmed.

3. **Peers use a familiar language register** and slang to talk about online activities that makes explanations, demonstrations, and modeling more accessible and comprehensible.

4. **Peer collaboration develops self-regulation** among group members, keeping each group member on task to plan, monitor, and evaluate online activities. In turn, this leads to the development of self-efficacy, an active learning environment, and a "can-do" attitude.

How Does Peer Collaboration Help the Development of Online Skills and Strategies?

A classroom culture that promotes a sense of community helps students develop self-efficacy and intrinsic motivation. It also aids students in setting learning-centered goals while building individual and situational interest within a self-regulated learning environment. These collaborative elements are keys toward fostering engagement in learning and reading outcomes and are developed by providing challenging and interesting learning activities, promoting student choice and autonomy, and inviting peers to engage in project-based work (Gambrell 1996; Guthrie and Wigfield 2000; Turner and Paris 1995). Peer collaboration is created by building a sense of community within the classroom culture, explicitly teaching online skills and strategies that students can adapt and make their own and by gradually releasing responsibility for the use of these skills and strategies to students as they read, write, and communicate online in meaningful ways.

How Can Teachers Create a Classroom Culture That Nurtures Collaboration?

There are a number of key factors central to the creation of a classroom culture that builds a sense of community within classrooms, encourages peer-to-peer collaboration, and helps the development of online skills and strategies. These features include:

- Constructing challenging inquiry-based activities
- Promoting student choice and autonomy
- Creating learner-centered goals
- Developing intrinsic motivation, self-efficacy, and self-regulation

Real world, authentic activities encourage problem solving, active thinking, involvement, and interest (Guthrie and Wigfield 2000). In the classroom, these activities often relate to integrated cross-curricular units drawn from across curriculum areas, which integrate literacy and the content areas of science, geography, history, and social studies. Examples of these cross-curricular units are discussed in a later section of this chapter. Some suggestions are included in Figure 7.1.

Figure 7. 1 Examples of Integrated Cross-Curricular Units

- Birds and Their Environments
- Animals' Adaptation to Their Environments
- Endangered Animals
- Investigating Scale in Outer Space and the Universe
- Exploring the Journey of Kites
- Voting Rights and Responsibilities
- Documenting our Communities

 Common Core to the Fore

An Integrated View of Literacy

The English Language Arts standards within the CCSS adopt an integrated view of literacy that recognizes the reciprocal processes of reading, writing, listening, and speaking (National Governors Association Center for Best Practices and Council of Chief State School Officers 2010). A defining feature of the CCSS is the inclusion of literacy across the curriculum at all grade levels and embedded within history/social studies, science, and technical subjects. The creation of this unique strand of standards has positioned literacy as the cornerstone of content learning by emphasizing literacy as a vital part of instruction within and across all content areas.

Setting the Context for Building Situational Interest

To develop situational interest and ultimately personal interest in cross-curricular topics of study, Guthrie (2004) suggests providing plenty of hands-on activities. Within these sorts of activities, which require the discussion and manipulation of objects, students expend more energy and persist to meet end goals. When tasks are personally relevant and interesting, this in turn engenders intrinsic motivation (Schiefele 1999). For example, in a unit related to birds and their environments, the teacher could invite a local birder into the classroom, students could observe the habits of birds when visiting bird tables in the school garden, and a video camera could be used to record and observe the habits of nestlings. Providing students with a choice of activities is a "powerful motivator" (Turner and Paris 1995). Initially, the teacher should provide guidance for students in making choices or provide a bounded set of options to choose from (Guthrie 2004).

It is also important to vary organizational strategies within the classroom. Students should be encouraged to collaborate in paired activities and group activities. Social collaboration enables students to position themselves within a community of learners in which the discussions that occur between students facilitate an increase in both individual and group confidence to succeed. As a result, students invest and persist in tasks as they socially construct meaning from text. Such social support can raise the bar for all group members by providing benchmarks of achievement and improvement within the group. Social support can also spark interest and curiosity and engender responsibility toward involving all group members. As students progress in their ability to apply strategies in whole-class and small-group settings, learning tasks can be designed to promote independent application.

Promoting Student Exchange of Internet Skills

Share boards, spaces where ideas are publicly displayed, can be used to support peer collaboration. They can be used in the classroom in two ways. First, they can be physical spaces, such as bulletin boards within the classroom, where students can share and alert other class members to the work they are conducting in an online environment. Dwyer (2010) found that share boards were an effective way to help students reflect on the types and kinds of focus questions they generate for online Internet inquiry. They can also be used for posting summaries of information obtained. Students can choose a question from a brainstormed list to place on a sticky note and locate on a bulletin board under the correct conceptual category. For example, in an inquiry-project based on animals' adaptations to their environment, one group asked the question, "Why do some sharks not eat meat?" and chose the conceptual category of *diet* from a list on the bulletin board titled *Feeding, Breathing, Moving, Reproduction, Growing, Adapting to Habitat*, and *Communication* (all topics were drawn from the science curriculum).

Second, share boards can be created in an online space using digital technologies. There are a number of digital tools, as previously discussed in Chapter 5, that can be used to generate electronic sticky notes to help students to dig deeper with questions and to promote social learning in the classroom. Further online spaces can be created using Google docs™ (https://docs.google.com), Nings (http://www.ning.com), or Wikispaces (http://www.wiki.com) where students can post their focus inquiry questions or summaries of information retrieved online to share with the class.

You may wonder about the advantages and disadvantages of the physical versus the electronic space for encouraging peer collaboration to reflect on inquiry-based questions and summaries in an inquiry-based classroom. Sometimes, the immediacy of a shared bulletin board in a space within the classroom provides a level of physicality not available in an online environment. On the other hand, the electronic environment provides a Web space for students to share and discuss inquiry-based questions in real time outside the four walls of the classroom. Whether in physical or electronic formats, share boards involve students in cognitive decision making and self-regulatory practices in a number of ways:

1. Students choose which one of their focus inquiry questions to post on the share board for their peers to see. Making this choice is helpful in promoting discussion about the types and kinds of questions asked.

2. Students must carefully reflect on and monitor the kinds of questions they ask to focus their Internet inquiry and the summaries of information obtained.

3. Share boards facilitate the sharing of useful websites and sources of online information among class members.

Class Discussions and Reflections

Class discussions and reflections are useful in facilitating share-outs that distribute knowledge about online skills and strategies, access and update prior knowledge sources, and monitor students' understanding of online strategies. Such class discussions can take place at the beginning of each Internet-inquiry session or at the end of a class when students can reflect on what strategies worked for them that day, what confused them, and what their learning goal for the next session would be. Class discussions help students to develop persistence, self-efficacy, motivation, and engagement within the group.

Short Inquiry Problems

Another way to promote discussions is to set up a routine for students to demonstrate different ways of addressing a short inquiry problem. For example, curriculum-based information challenges are short, teacher-designed activities that invite students to respond collaboratively to a question or problem related to a unit of study (Castek 2008). Inviting students to address the challenge in collaboration with a partner invites an authentic exchange of ideas as students work to gather information online to find a solution to the challenge posed. Providing students with a very limited amount of time (20 minutes or less) to complete the challenge ensures that they will work efficiently and build on one another's ideas. When time is up, students can be invited to share the processes used to address the challenge. In the early stages, the teacher can model a new strategy that students can then use independently or adapt to new situations. Over time, students can be invited to demonstrate solutions in front of the class and model the processes they used. Completing these challenges creates opportunities for students to collaborate and exchange ideas with others who possessed varying levels of skills and experience in using the Internet.

Short inquiry problems can be focused with broad categories of searching for information, evaluating information, synthesizing information, or communicating information. An example of a short inquiry problem focused on evaluating information follows.

> *The teacher writes the following prompt on the board. "What caused the downfall of California's Velcro® crops?*

In this example, students use the search terms "California Velcro® crops" and ultimately end up at a website entitled, California's Velcro® Crop Under Challenge (see Appendix B for URL). Once there, students begin to summarize that crops are failing due to drought, disease, and pests. Then, students are prompted to use their prior knowledge of what Velcro® is (a human-made plastic that's used as a fastener for clothing and footwear), and they often begin a conversation about whether Velcro® could be grown at all. Using strategies such as reading about the author, attempting to verify the information found here on other websites, and visiting http://snopes.com (a source for urban legends, myths, rumors, and misinformation), students begin to determine that this is a spoof website that contains bogus information. Engaging in the process reminds students to check the veracity of information they read online, an essential higher-level thinking strategy when reading online information.

 ## Common Core to the Fore

Promoting Higher-Level Thinking

In order to take advantage of the resources the Internet makes available, students must become skilled at selecting, evaluating, managing, and organizing information resources effectively and efficiently. Many of these higher-order online reading comprehension skills appear in the CCSS and will be essential for success in both literacy and content-area classrooms. In addition, the CCSS call for extended collaboration in which learners build on other's ideas, express their own ideas, pose questions, elaborate, acknowledge new information, and modify their views. As today's students become more reliant on the Internet as a context for learning, and the CCSS call for a focus on higher-level thinking, it is imperative that educators across grade levels provide supported opportunities to engage in online reading that involves Internet searching and the examination of a range of online resources. Such activities not only support online reading skills and strategies but they also provide a motivational and authentic conversation that promotes productive collaboration (Castek, Coiro, Guzniczak, and Bradshaw 2012).

Quick Shares

Quick shares refer to those "Aha!" moments when students discover a particularly effective website, an answer to a puzzling question, a new search strategy, an effective search string, or a new clue to watch for in the search result abstract. These fleeting moments need to be shared in that instant to consolidate effective strategies across the class group. Students can alert the teacher of their need to have a quick share, and the teacher can facilitate this within the class group.

Building Peer Collaboration: Developing the Online Reciprocal Roles

Peer-to-peer collaboration in an online environment does not always occur spontaneously; therefore, structures need to be put in place to encourage students to share and exchange ideas, insights, and strategies (Dwyer 2010). Reciprocal Teaching (Palincsar and Brown 1984) is a well-researched and validated instructional model. The teacher engages the students in a teacher-led dialogue in which instructional strategies are explicitly modeled and are embedded in meaningful contexts. This is followed by a gradual release of responsibility to the students so that they take turns in leading the dialogue centered on one of the reciprocal teaching roles of questioning, predicting, clarifying, and summarizing. In an online environment, the "more knowledgeable other" within the classroom may not always be the classroom teacher, and adopting reciprocal-teaching methods is one way to ensure that students can both lead and share developing online strategies. In an online environment, reciprocal roles could include students taking on the roles of *Navigator*, *Questioner*, and *Summarizer* (Dwyer 2010). The Questioner (a) guides the group to formulate higher-level questions to focus online inquiry and (b) directs, generates, discusses, and monitors the effectiveness of search terms for the focus inquiry. The Navigator (a) pilots the group to move effectively and efficiently in traversing multiple websites, and (b) encourages the group to carefully scrutinize the search results by examining the clues provided in the abstract blurb and URL and matching both to the focus of inquiry. The Summarizer (a) ensures that the group judged the relevance of the information retrieved by the group to the focus inquiry question, (b) encourages the group to monitor and clarify difficult vocabulary, and (c) guides the group in encapsulating and summarizing the information generated by the Internet inquiry. In Figure 7.2, fifth-grade students explain their understanding of the roles of Questioner, Navigator, and Summarizer.

Figure 7.2 Voices of the Students

 ## Voices from the Classroom

Let's listen to the voices of fifth-grade students as they explain their understanding of what is involved in each of these online reciprocal roles:

The Navigator "is a finder or clicker. They scan the [results] page and decide what to click into [as the] first one [hyperlink] might be good but the last one might be better."

The Questioner "Their job is to make the question that you want to find out...shorten the search terms, so it won't be too broad...use the plus sign it tells the computer that you want the two of them."

The Summarizer "pull the most important thing, put it in your own words and size it down [and] say what it's about in one sentence... some of the words might be in dark print so you know to use them... and see the words we don't understand."

Dwyer 2010

Introducing Online Reciprocal Roles

First, brainstorm with students what each of these roles may entail. If students have used the print-based reciprocal roles of predicting, summarizing, clarifying, and questioning or the literature circle roles (Daniels 2002) of Artful Artist, Passage Picker, Connector, and Questioner, they could draw on this prior knowledge in constructing the possibilities.

Second, the roles can be introduced one at a time, using the Gradual Release of Responsibility model outlined earlier. Sample prompt cards, such as those displayed in Figure 7.3, can be placed on key rings and used as scaffolds to remind individuals of their roles within groups. Of course, the roles should be swapped around to ensure the overall development of the skills and strategies necessary for successful online inquiry. As with all scaffolds, the prompt cards are temporary aids and become redundant as students internalize the necessary skills and strategies and develop proficiency with each of the online roles.

Figure 7.3 Sample Prompt Cards for the Roles of Questioner, Navigator, and Summarizer

Navigator	Questioner	Summarizer
Which link should we follow?	What are we trying to find out today?	What's the most important information here?
Will we read the blurb under each search result?	How will we pick our keywords? What are our keywords?	Let's skim and scan to see if this website is useful for our question.
Will we scroll down the page?	Are there any other words we could choose for our search term?	What would we tell our friend?

Dwyer 2010

The following ideas demonstrate how the use of online reciprocal roles facilitates the development of Internet-inquiry skills and strategies.

- The prompt cards act as temporary scaffolds of the roles and help students apply the reading strategies of questioning, navigating, and summarizing to structure the online-inquiry activities in groups. When the students have internalized the strategies encompassed in these roles, the cards may be discarded.

- The roles help students to self-initiate problem solving within a group. The discussions within the peer-to-peer interactions help students initiate, explain, clarify, justify, negotiate, challenge thinking, problem-solve, and resolve disputes within group activities.

- The roles also help students stay on task, direct online activities, and self-regulate their reading activities. The roles also support the development of conceptual understanding and strategic processing within the group.

- The roles develop shifting leadership positions within group activities. During peer-to-peer exchanges, the more "knowledgeable other" (Vygotsky 1978) is dynamic and shifts as students problem solve by drawing on a range of prior knowledge sources.

- The roles provide a structured framework to encourage consensus and engender a sense of shared responsibility in conducting Internet inquiry within a group activity.

- The roles enable successful completion of a task through collective problem solving, including revision of strategies. Students will come to see that "What I can do with others today, I can do on my own tomorrow."

- The roles also provide an opportunity for students to reflect on their learning within the group. Strategies such as Rate My Role, using a scale of 1 (not great) to 5 (awesome), are useful to help students to self- and peer-assess. Each assigned score must be justified through discussion. As such, it is the reflection on why they assigned a particular score rather than the score itself per se that is valuable for individuals within the group, the group itself, and the classroom teacher.

Extending Collaboration

The Internet has become today's technology for literacy and learning, offering classrooms a wide range of reading options that include online interactions with learners outside the classroom community. Online reading, writing, and communication activities provide new opportunities for social interaction and collaboration with others (Boling et al. 2008; Zawilinski 2009). Online participation motivates students to read for a range of purposes, utilize knowledge gained from previous experience to generate new understandings, and actively engage in meaningful interactions around reading. Learning activities that integrate peer collaboration fulfill an important need since many students, especially adolescents, are driven by social interaction. One such indication is the proliferation of teen activity on social-networking sites (Lenhart et al. 2007).

Many adolescents spend their time connecting with friends by texting on cell phones, instant messaging, and using websites such as Facebook, Instagram, and Twitter®. Just a 10-minute peek at the flurry of activity that occurs when an adolescent logs into Facebook helps us to recognize how skilled today's adolescents are with dynamically creating their own communities and establishing affinity groups within those networks to connect with others and exchange ideas on any number of topics.

Providing opportunities to communicate and collaborate with their peers from other schools nationally and globally helps to broaden students' points of view and teaches them different ways to approach and solve problems. Online learning networks allow students to collaborate by using tools such as email, blogs, wikis, and other networking platforms to create, invent, and showcase their work. These tools, when chosen thoughtfully and implemented in conjunction with instruction in online reading comprehension, can become fertile ground for students acquiring the skills necessary to communicate and collaborate in a global marketplace.

In the sections that follow, we suggest ways to build collaboration skills through implementation of:

- online book clubs

- email exchanges

- collaborative Internet projects

- online shared writing projects

Online Book Clubs

Online book clubs celebrate great books by assembling a diverse audience to discuss and appreciate them. In2books Clubhouse promotes sharing ideas about books and invites students of all ages to simultaneously participate in book discussions (see Appendix B for URL). Students discuss their favorite books and authors, submit short stories and poetry, and share the books they love with others. Planet Book Talk makes it possible for students to read comments other students have posted about books, access book reviews written by kids of all ages, or post their own comments or reviews (see Appendix B for URL). Participation can promote higher-level thinking, communication skills, and deeper understandings of text. Integrating such activities into the classroom provides strong social reasons for reading because these activities involve a process of constructing meanings and sharing them with others. Each of these unique sites shows that communities of readers are flourishing online and that these networks are bringing people together around books like never before.

Email Exchanges

Many educators are unaware of projects that use email for classroom collaboration. The ePals™ Global Community (http://www.epals.com/) connects classrooms around the world by offering safe, teacher monitored email accounts. Because these resources are free and easy to use, more than 133,000 classrooms have participated in ePals™ email exchanges. Teachers can easily prescreen students' accounts, making it possible to spot problems and encourage positive communication. Integrating email exchanges into your classroom program is particularly powerful in providing authentic purposes for sharing ideas, using language, and developing literacy among students of all ages. For example, a rural class in the United States might connect with an urban class and discuss issues related to transportation. Because ePals™ registers classes from all over the world, these forums encourage readers to consider diverse opinions and think in new ways.

The ePals™ Student Forum is a student-centered discussion board organized by topics such as *Arts and Entertainment, Global Issues/Current Events*, and *Looking for Information on…*. Students can access email threads of interest, post their own opinions, ask for advice, or present new ideas (see Appendix B for URL). This is also a way for students to learn how to ask good questions.

An additional resource for encouraging an exchange of ideas between students about issues of the day is Voices Of Youth® (http://www.voicesofyouth.org). This forum seeks to empower youth to use dialogue to seek solutions for today's most pressing global problems. In this discussion area, students can dialogue and reflect on world issues relating to human rights, the environment, violence, war, and conflict, to name a few.

In2Books is designed to foster reading and writing skills in grades 3–5 (see Appendix A for URL). This site matches students in your class with an adult email pal who is carefully screened and trained to support student learning. Each pair reads the same five books and exchanges emails to prompt a rich discussion about the content, characters, choices, and theme. The online dialogue generates enthusiasm for reading and encourages conversation about literature. A study conducted by Teale and Gambrell (2007) demonstrated wide-scale positive effects on students' literacy learning.

Internet Projects

Participation in collaborative Internet projects creates new definitions of reading and writing that transform school-based learning into events that are meaningful, real world, and social. Promoting collaboration among communities of learners that extend far beyond the classroom walls creates authentic reasons to share ideas. By supporting students' engagement in collaborative activities, educators capitalize on the appeal and motivation of connecting worldwide. Through these efforts, students can assess situations, take global trends into consideration, and ultimately participate in finding solutions that may impact the realities of tomorrow. Visit the iEARN Collaboration Center, The Teacher's Collaboration Projects, or the United Nations Cyber School Bus to locate Internet projects that involve students in issues of global concern (see Appendix B for URLs). These projects support finding solutions to combat world hunger, ending racial and ethnic discrimination, and providing universal human rights. Placing students in the role of problem solvers empowers them to find ways to use what they are learning in school and their communities to change the reality of the world around them.

Furthermore, ePals offers easy-to-implement projects for classroom collaboration such as *Weather Watchers, Become Detectives,* and others that teachers have designed (e.g., *Endangered Animals Extinction Project, Green Campus Project,* and *International Calendar Project*) to intersect with a variety of topics across the curriculum. Participation in such collaborative projects promotes teamwork, reinforces Internet reading and writing skills, and makes it possible for students to see themselves, their abilities, and activities at school in a different light. Not only does this give students the opportunity to affect change in the world and gain valuable experience with the new forms of online communication that are quickly defining our world, but it also builds confidence that the skills they are learning have value beyond the classroom.

Online Writing Projects

Cross-classroom writing projects unite students in exploring common topics (Leu 2002). These projects can be housed on a *wiki*—a collaborative writing space that makes it easy to share resources, co-construct ideas, and dialogue about the writing process. In the following Classroom Connection, students worked together to research national parks in the United States, find out about the activities each park offered, and create a wiki page about each park. The final product was a collection of persuasive pieces designed to encourage fifth-grade students to visit one of the parks. The project was designed to give students experience co-constructing ideas and to demonstrate the benefits of collaborating with classroom partners within and outside the four walls of the classroom.

 # Classroom Connection

Collaborative Writing on a Wiki

In this project, students were introduced to the concept of a wiki and its features. They worked in pairs to co-construct a wiki entry on a national park as a collaborative writing project. Pairs collaborated virtually with a class at another school to compose, edit, and revise the entries. They used the comment features on the wiki to discuss ideas with their partner class that they then included in their writing. Students tracked the history of the wiki pages they created to see how their entries evolved over time through the process of collaboration.

First, the teacher introduced the concept of a wiki. Then, she presented students with a collaboration request from a class in San Francisco and showed them a digital photo of their partner class. She introduced a wiki page about national parks and explained that students would work in pairs to create a page on the wiki about a national park (about five sentences with a picture). Then, students in the partner class would read the entries and add onto the information, revising what was written and reorganizing the ideas in order to improve the entry. The goal of each group was to write a wiki that would convince other fifth-grade students to visit their national park.

The teacher showed students an example of a completed wiki page:

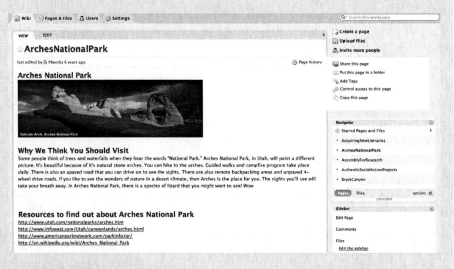

Printed with permission from Jill Castek

The teacher demonstrated for students how to use the "Edit Page" button to revise, change, or add new information on to the page, how to use the "Save" button to record the changes, and how to use the "Comments" feature to pose a question or make a request of the other class.

The class revised a sample entry together as an example of how to use the specific features, using the following steps:

Step 1. Choose a national park from a list, or receive an assigned park from the teacher.

Step 2. Explore Internet sites about your park.

Step 3. Read what students from the partner class have started writing about each of the parks, telling the special qualities, location, and best sights to see in each park. Some have included a picture.

Step 4. Revise, edit, and add ideas to what other students have already started. Make your page as convincing as possible to get a student to visit your park.

Step 5. Read the comments that go with each page. This is where the other class has included questions or requests for which they would like a response. You can discuss your writing ideas with students from the other class, using the comments section.

Step 6. Save the changes to your page when you are done.

Students then set to work on their wiki pages as the teacher observed closely to look for instances of unique strategy use. When she observed these unique strategies, she noted them and asked students if they would be willing to demonstrate and talk about these strategies in front of the class.

Students tracked the development of the wiki pages with great interest and looked forward to collaborating with students in the other class as they shared comments, provided suggestions, and edited one another's work.

Final Thoughts on Collaboration

In this chapter, we have explored ways to promote quality collaboration among students, structures for supporting collaboration in classrooms, and instructional activities that facilitate collaboration. We have suggested that promoting peer interaction among learners as they engage in online literacy can help students to co-construct knowledge and thereby generate higher-quality work than individuals working alone. We have found that encouraging students to collaboratively share online reading and writing strategies with one another not only aids the receiver of the information, but it also helps students who act as the teacher. The "in-the-moment" assistance offered during peer collaboration supports students in applying online-literacy strategies more widely and will ultimately lead students to a more nuanced understanding of how and when to use a broad array of online-literacy strategies independently.

Questions for Reflection

1. The strategies discussed in this chapter help to promote a classroom culture that fosters the exchange of Internet reading, writing, and communication strategies among students. Which of them would you like to try in your classroom?

2. Social collaboration does not occur spontaneously. What strategies are discussed that help build productive peer collaboration among students? How can you use these in your instructions?

3. What skills can students learn through extended opportunities to use digital technologies in collaboration with their peers? In what ways are these skills beneficial within and beyond school?

4. How does co-constructing ideas with other students and participating in forums such as online book clubs, email exchanges, and online writing projects promote the skills required for effective collaboration?

CHAPTER 8

Strategies for Building Communities of Writers

In this chapter, you will learn:

- strategies for using several digital-writing tools to support students' expression of ideas in multiple forms;

- techniques for supporting the writing process using collaborative writing applications; and

- ways to organize your classroom to support the use of digital writing tools.

After reading this chapter, you will:

- understand the important reasons why digital writing engages students in the writing process;

- draw insights about the collaborative writing process that can be easily facilitated with the help of digital tools; and

- be prepared to experiment with a digital-writing experience using digital-tools features.

Exploring the Affordances of Digital Writing

Internet technologies are rapidly changing the landscape of reading and writing. The increased availability of inexpensive digital devices has made technology use ubiquitous and fundamental to all aspects of our daily life. In the process, these devices have transformed the ways we communicate and share ideas.

While new technologies have made it possible for students to embrace digital composition as a means of self-expression, a significant gap exists between the way young people employ technology in their personal lives and the literacy instruction they receive in the classroom (O'Brien and Scharber 2008). Recognizing the disconnect between students' everyday literacy practices and the classroom reading and writing they often participate in at school is an important first step toward transforming writing instruction. The next step is providing multiple means by which students can craft exchanges to share ideas with the outside world. For example, mobile technologies allow students to move around freely as they compose, collect photographs or other artifacts to include in digital compositions, and bring in elements of their voice through representations of their daily world.

Digital writing, multimodal composition, and video production help students develop, organize, and present information. Final products can convey messages through a variety of modalities. These digitally enhanced experiences embrace an expanded view of literacy that positions writing as an act of communication that extends beyond alphabetic-only compositions to include digital compositions incorporating video, images, animation, sound effects, and voice narration as well as text as a means of expressing ideas.

Digital composition that involves drawing with voice narration or video creation remains largely absent from digital-classroom activities. The focus on producing alphabetic-only products, whether digital or paper and pencil, creates a gap of untapped potential. It is our responsibility as teachers to provide an educational context in which all students can participate in multimodal writing experiences to open new avenues for self-expression. Giving students these opportunities to create digital content is central to guiding them to become participatory citizens who are well versed in academic language and able to achieve success in school, higher education, and the workplace.

Video Production as a Form of Digital Writing

Sixth-graders, Carlos and Jasmine, talk excitedly as they create an iMovie® on the iPad® in their science class. "Let's make sure we emphasize that California sits on a transform boundary. We can put in an image of the coast and draw arrows showing the Pacific plate moving north and the North American plate moving south. Then, we can add our voice-over and tell more about plate movement on the fault line," Jasmine suggests. "Yeah, then we can add in a video clip," Carlos adds, "so when we edit everything together. It explains how the plates catch on each other and jerk suddenly during an earthquake." Throughout the process, students show an awareness of their viewing audience and refine their work accordingly.

Their teacher, Mr. Young, looks on and nods. It is evident his students are engaged and eager to share what they've learned about plate tectonics. He has recognized that creating videos requires that students work collaboratively to plan, compose, and revise to communicate a clear message. He knows this has helped his students deepen their science understanding while at the same time enhancing their literacy and digital communication skills. He is enthusiastic about the potential of video creation to help students express their understanding in a creative, interactive, and transformative way.

Common Core to the Fore

Expanding What Counts as Writing

The CCSS calls for learners to become skilled at writing and presenting ideas using technology. For example, students are expected to use technology, including the Internet, to produce, publish, and interact with others about writing while also recognizing the strengths and limitations of various technological tools. They are also expected to select and skillfully use digital tools that are suited to meeting specific communication goals. In addition, learners are expected to engage in opportunities that utilize traditional forms of print, digital, and online reading and writing and represent various genres and perspectives, as well as media and communication technologies. Positioning writing in this way widens the scope of classroom-writing experiences and supports students' development and communication of ideas across the curriculum. An increased emphasis on technology use in the Common Core State Standards has paved the way for students' use of digital devices in the classroom. This opens up new potential to engage students in digital-composition experiences across the curriculum.

Planning for Writing: Mind Maps and Thinking Tools

Concept mapping helps students visually represent logical or causal relationships between ideas associated with a certain phenomenon. Using concept-mapping apps, students identify a variety of keywords associated with an experience, a topic, or an issue and visually organize the logical relationships among these words. Students may insert the words into circles or boxes, draw lines or spokes between ideas, and insert subtopics. These connecting lines serve to define the logical relationships among ideas. For example, it can be determined whether a sub-topic serves as an illustrative example of a major topic. Within many concept-mapping applications, students can create an outline list of words with subcategories within those words, and the application will then generate different types of maps using these outlines. Many concept-mapping tools also include the affordances of color-coding different ideas as a means of visually representing different categories of information. Student examples can be found in Figure 8.1.

Figure 8.1 Student Concept Maps for "What Is Gold?" Created in Popplet

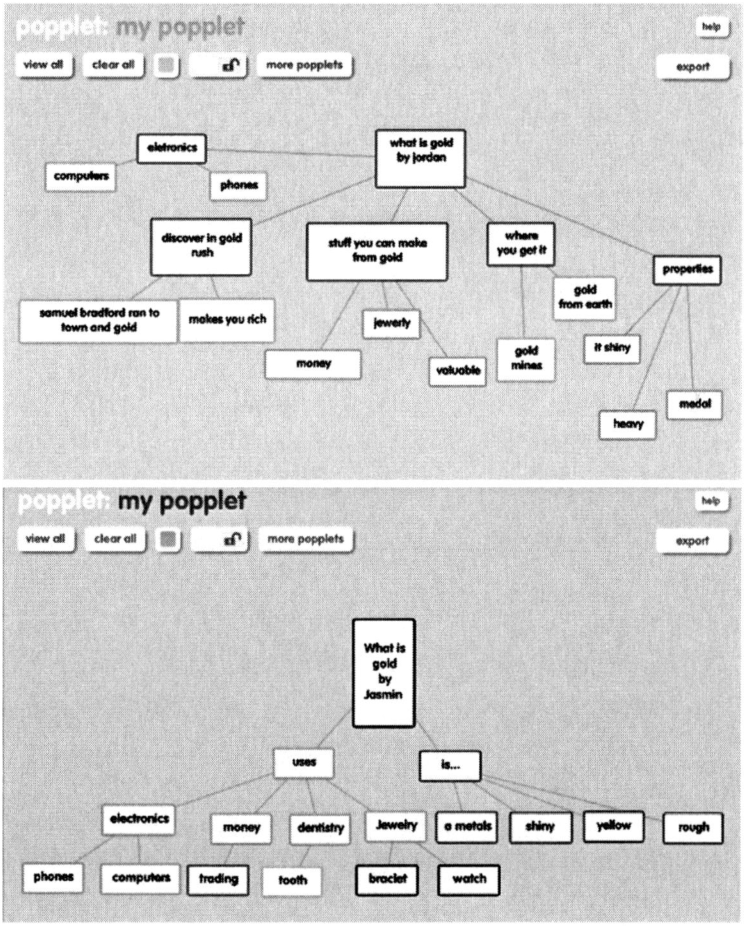

Printed with permission from Popplet

Digital concept-mapping applications serve to help students collaboratively develop and expand topics. By sharing the same concept maps, a group of students working on the same project can visually represent their thinking for one another so that they are literally and figuratively "on the same page." Students can then pose questions of one another based on their maps, for example, questions about connections between ideas or the need for more information to solidify understanding of a topic. While concept mapping can also be accomplished using paper and pencil, revision capabilities are limited. In the digital form, substantial changes can be made effortlessly, making revision more palatable to students.

Students can also use their maps to define an overall focus for their project. While students' maps may begin with a limited number of ideas, they may recognize that their focus has shifted as they develop other sections of their maps. This shift in attention signals the need for revision to alter their overall focus.

Composing Using Multimedia Tools

Digital tools are transforming what it means to be literate in today's world. In the past, decoding words on a page may have been enough to consider a student literate. Today, we live in a world with ever-increasing importance on digital tools and technologies as a means of accessing and sharing ideas. Having the ability to comprehend, critically respond to, and collaboratively compose multimodal texts will play a central role in our students' success in a digital-information age (Partnership for 21st Century Skills 2007; IRA 2009). As a result, students must become facile with the full range of communicative tools, modes (oral and written), and media.

While digital devices are a great way for students to access content in dynamic ways such as viewing videos and animations, taking virtual field trips, and reading eTexts, they also provide a diversity of methods to create content. Providing students the means to plan, design, and produce projects that use digital tools further extends learning. They provide the means for students to generate their own representations that demonstrate what they have learned in innovative ways that tap into their creativity. Designing digital compositions calls on students to think across modes of representation that can include text as well as images, sounds, and music in ways that transcend paper-and-pencil products. The ability to record a voice-over script extends the composition process, making the final message come to life.

A myriad of applications for digital content creation in the classroom are readily available. Three of these include iMovie® (http://apple.com/apps/imovie/), a video creation app that makes shooting and editing a video a snap, ShowMe (http://showme.com), an app that lets you create a storyboard with images and drawing and includes a voice-over feature, and VoiceThread® (http://voicethread.com), a collaborative multimedia-slide show that holds images and allows creators or viewers to add voice-over commentary. The creativity that students infuse throughout multimedia writing projects reminds us that harnessing students' potential for humor and creativity digitally can enhance their communicative ability and writing skills (see Appendix B for URLs).

Remixing: Weaving Collective Ideas Together into a Single Text

Laura is a teacher at a charter school in Oakland, California, who is committed to writing across the curriculum. This Classroom Connection showcases how she engaged her fifth graders in a collaborative-writing project she designed to incorporate disciplinary writing into a science unit. Her aim was to explore how digital technologies could be used to support students' engagement, self-expression, and science learning. By using the web-based collaborative MixedInk™ platform, she supported collaborative writing in her classroom.

Classroom Connection

Designing the Writing Assignment

With the help of Stop Waste and Waste Management of Alameda County, fifth-graders in Oakland, California, engaged in a waste audit to analyze the garbage their school produced. Their new learning sparked an interest in encouraging the school community to become more mindful about their output of trash and how to sort their trash better.

As an introduction into the collaborative-writing assignment, students discussed their experiences with the waste audit and shared ideas about how to communicate the surprising results they found to the school and community at large. In this way, the students themselves defined their audience, which created an authentic context for writing. As a result, students invested in their writing as a means of communicating ideas that were important to them.

The teacher, Laura, structured a five-paragraph writing frame that mirrored the components of a scientific lab report and assigned each table group one paragraph of the final product to complete. The structure and organization of the final piece was then presented to the students so they could see how their contribution would fit into the completed whole. The first paragraph provided background about the trash audit, the second provided information about the science ideas students had been learning, the third discussed the recycling facilities in Alameda County and how much waste and recycled materials are collected annually, the fourth provided raw data about what students found during the audit, and the fifth summarized what the school community could do to become more green. The graphic organizers scaffolded students in drafting their specific paragraph. Before writing, Laura encouraged table groups to discuss ideas using the guiding questions she provided on the graphic organizer. Then, students completed a first draft.

Exploring the Collaborative Writing Platform

Having used a wiki for collaborative writing in the past, Laura was excited to try a new tool to facilitate collaborative writing and located a free platform called MixedInk™ (http://www.mixedink.com). This educator-friendly tool allows small groups or the whole class to draft and reflect on several versions of a text written on the same topic and to weave ideas from peers' work into a single text that credits multiple authors. An overview of how the MixedInk™ tool works can be seen in the short video clip available on the MixedInk™ website (see Appendix B for URL). Below are the steps involved, adapted from the MixedInk™ site.

1. **Write, edit, and remix:** Students write together and then create their own versions, edit their peers' work, and combine different versions into new ones.

2. **Comment and evaluate:** Students comment on their classmates' writing and rate different versions to identify the best language and ideas.

3. **Discuss the top version as a class:** The class explores their favorite texts together.

Not only is each aspect an important part of productive-collaborative writing, but these steps also address the Common Core State Standards that emphasize the use of digital technologies for reading and writing and support process skills such as collaboration, listening, and speaking.

Students learned about the process of collaborative writing by viewing the *MixedInk™ for Educators* video as a class. They discussed peer support for adding content, revising language choices, and reorganizing the presentation of ideas. After the video, questions emerged, and the differences between collaborative writing (in which all authors are credited) and plagiarizing (taking someone's ideas and passing them off as their own) were clarified. As is often the case when presenting a new digital tool, students readily picked up on the site organization and the available features and posed questions about options. These questions prompted exploration and student-to-student sharing when the time came for students to use the tool.

Reading and Rating

Once students inputted their drafts into MixedInk™, they read and rated one another's work using a star system that ranged on a scale from *excellent* to *needs work*. The classes then discussed the process of peer support for adding content, revising language choices, and reorganizing their presentation of ideas. As students read their peers' work, they critiqued the writing not only with the intent of verifying science content and ideas but also with an eye toward gathering language, sentence structures, and ideas that could be incorporated from their peers' work into a new collaborative draft. Students were aware that borrowing from other students' pieces created a shared text in which all authors were credited.

Remixing

Using their peers' pieces as mentor texts, students remixed new drafts by incorporating elements of one another's wording and language into their own piece, in the process creating co-written pieces with multiple authors. MixedInk™ uses a color-coded crediting process where each author is recognized as a contributing author. MixedInk™ tracks each student's contribution to the collaboratively written piece. Different colors represent each individual's work.

School Waste Letter Paragraph 5

Rate: Paragraph 5

👤 show authors   ✏️ edit this   🗐 add to notes   💬 comment   ⚠️ report

We think the school should STOP and LISTEN. We should use reusable containers for food, not ziplock bags and eat wastefree lunch.Bring containers and metal reuseable water bottles.We think Lighthouse should consider this data carefully and see how we can improve.We think you should take our data seriously by telling this to other students at other schools about how to reuse and recycle things because we don't want to live in an environment that is filled with trash everywhere. We say this because our data as you saw before, showed that 75% could have been diverted. That's more than what can be diverted at the Altamont landfill which says that 63% of the waste there could have been diverted. We should recycle , reuse cartons, to reduce,and rot to help plants be healthy.If it rots, let it rot for a garden.We should go class to class and to do a presentation that talks about the 4R's and explain what they are to do with food.My final idea is that we should teach kids and classes to save the planet.SO REMEMBER always reuse,reduce,recycle and rot.So this is why we should recycle, reuse, rot, and reduce.Lets use the 4R'S more often!

Add a comment   View comments (1)

Printed with permission from MixedInk

Rating Remixed Drafts

After remixing, students then engaged in a second round of rating. MixedInk™ employs a specially designed algorithm that identified the most complete and well-written piece, based on students' ratings. This featured version can then be discussed in terms of its organization, use of language, or other characteristics. With help from the students, Laura compiled the top-rated five paragraphs into a completed piece that incorporated all students' voices. The final version took full advantage of the collaborative writing process in the creation of a well-organized, well-structured final product.

LIGHTHOUSE COMMUNITY CHARTER SCHOOL
GUIDING EVERY CHILD TO A BRIGHT FUTURE

February 7, 2012

Dear Staff and Faculty,

We are 5th grade garbologists in Ms. Kretschmar's math and science class. That means we study garbage. The question we asked was how much of our waste at school could be diverted from the landfill to be recycled or composted. Our hypothesis was 50% of the waste at Lighthouse Community Charter School could be diverted from going to the landfill. We worked with StopWaste.org to investigate 5 random trash bags from our dumpster. We separated the trash into three bins: recycle, compost, and landfill. This is called a waste audit. We are telling you this because we want you to have this information so you can help stop waste!

The big scientific idea behind our investigation and waste audit that matter is neither created nor destroyed. People think that when they throw the waste in the garbage, it just disappears. It doesn't. When people say, "Let's throw this away," what they don't realize is that the waste can sometimes get reused, reduced, recycled, or it can rot. Reuse means instead of throwing something away, keep on using it. Reduce means using less of something. Recycle means when a product gets transformed into a similar or different product to be used again. Finally, rot is when something decomposes. If we don't practice the 4 Rs, some unnecessary waste is piled up in the landfill. We don't want any more waste that could have been recycled or composted in the landfill because it takes up space. Also, if we use the four Rs then our school, homes, and community can be cleaner.

Did you know there are 1,500,000 people in Alameda County? That is a lot of waste that is neither created nor destroyed. Five to six pounds of trash are thrown out per person in our county each day. Five pounds is like a bin of books that we have in the classes. When the trash gets picked up from houses and schools it goes to the Davis Transfer Station. From the Davis Transfer Station it goes to the Altamont Landfill in Livermore. The Altamont Landfill is the size of 2000 football fields. About 63% of the garbage there could have been composted or recycled.

Now, back to our waste audit data. The three main categories we sorted were compost, landfill, and recycle. The type of waste we mostly found in our trash was soda cans, chip bags, water bottles, paper bags, food, flowers, coffee cups, plastic containers. We found that 70% of our school waste can be diverted from the Altamont Landfill (our hypothesis was only 50%!). Our data was higher than the Altamont Landfill data, and our hypothesis, because our data was 70% and the Landfill data was 63%.

We think Lighthouse should consider this data carefully and see how we can improve. Lighthouse needs to wake up. We have different ideas to reduce, reuse, recycle, and rot. One idea is to do presentations and go to each class to talk about where our waste goes, how we are not throwing things away properly, and how we must improve. With your permission we would like to visit your class or crew to make a five-minute presentation of this data and our recommendations. Ms. Kretschmar will contact you, or you can contact us through her, with any questions.

Thank you, and have a good day.

The 5th Grade Garbologists

P.S.   We used a program called http://www.mixedink.com/#/_how_it_works to collaboratively write this letter. Each person wrote different paragraphs—then we mixed and matched sentences that we liked from each other's paragraphs through mixed ink and put the letter together!

P.S.S. We asked Ms. K to email this or post this on the blog to practice one of the Rs—Reduce Paper!

Printed with permission from Laura Kretschmar

Reflecting on the Writing Process

When asked about making these digital products, students said the work was "fun and cooperative." Not only did collaboration support engagement with content, but it also supported the development of vital 21st Century literacies. Students were able to showcase their learning in ways that involved the development of voice and self-expression, which requires higher-level thinking skills such as synthesis, evaluation, and critique, which are also central to the Common Core State Standards.

Reading through a remixed piece with multiple authors combines different students' ideas and provides for a level of reflection that supports the development of writing skills. This allowed learners to view and examine the elements that were incorporated into the final collaborative piece with the intent of encouraging the inclusion of these elements into their future written pieces.

Reflecting on the Lesson

Laura learned that collaborative writing is a process that draws upon the strengths of the collective. Although one student may be stronger in critical-thinking skills, another may excel in organizing ideas, adding detail, or incorporating in precise vocabulary. By working in groups to write collaboratively, students learn from one another while they write in ways that benefit both the individual and the whole group.

The act of collaboration encourages students to take advantage of group members for the purpose of peer review throughout the writing process. More and more workplace activities involve working in these sorts of collaborative-project teams. Giving students opportunities to work collaboratively can help prepare them for the advantages and pitfalls of collaborative work on the job.

We have seen collaborative-writing activities such as the one featured in this vignette support students' abilities to work together and problem-solve while maintaining a sense of ownership and accomplishment. The content-rich conversations that are invoked by such work are further evidence of the power of a collaborative nature when delivering writing instruction.

Collaborative Resourcing: Sharing Links and Annotations

Students' ability to engage in close reading, or focusing attention on and reviewing specific information, is a critical literacy skill involved in understanding texts, especially texts found in science and social studies. Students can use note-taking/annotation apps such as Evernote®, Diigo®, iAnnotate®, or DocAS to target specific information and summarize key claims or findings (see Appendix B for URLs). When students use digital annotations to raise or pose their own questions, they have the ability to build on one another's questions with their own annotations and are exposed to alternative responses that may differ from their own, resulting in their appropriation of new ways to interpret texts (Coiro, Castek, and Guzniczak 2011). This sort of perspective-taking involves recognizing alternative claims and the evidence that supports them while also thinking through counterclaims that refute alternative explanations.

Classroom Connection

Collaborative Annotation Tools in Action

Seventh-graders in Melanie's science classes at a charter school in Oakland, CA used the Diigo® annotation tool to examine the pros and cons of wind energy. Diigo® (http://www.diigo.com) is a social bookmarking/annotation app that allows students to annotate by posing questions and making connections across texts and annotations.

Students were provided with two articles—a pro article arguing that wind power has a number of positive benefits and a con article arguing that wind power is not cost effective. Students used the Diigo® social bookmarking/annotation app and Web highlighter to mark up the articles. The Diigo® tool allows students to add annotations as sticky notes right within the Web text they're reading.

In this lesson, students posed questions and made reflections and connections to ideas within the text. Diigo® also has a collaboration feature that allows students to share their sticky-note annotations within their own classroom group. As students engaged in inquiry by responding to texts, they were often encouraged to collaboratively test out competing claims and find supporting evidence to support those claims.

While Melanie's instinct was to model elements of the apps that students could embed and use in their projects, she resisted this tendency. As project work unfolded, it became increasingly clear that experimentation with the digital tools supported student learning more efficiently.

More and more workplace activities involve working in these sorts of collaborative project teams, and giving students opportunities to work together ensures that they will be well-prepared for such projects.

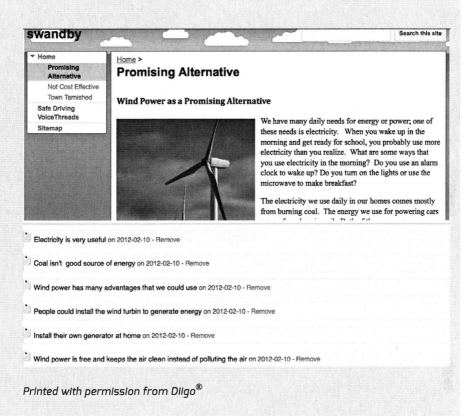

Printed with permission from Diigo®

Final Thoughts on Strategies for Building Communities of Writers

Teachers can use examples from this chapter to influence their own digital-teaching methods. It is our hope that your efforts will move beyond simple word processing toward the implementation of collaborative writing and construction of text that integrate multimodal elements such as image, sound, and video. In the process, you will demonstrate that you value different forms of self-expression while allowing students to use and learn their emerging 21st Century digital literacies to communicate ideas. It is our responsibility as teachers to provide an educational context in which all students can participate in these experiences.

Questions for Reflection

1. How can communication be expanded through the use of digital tools?

2. In what ways can the use of digital tools support students' writing development?

3. How might reluctant writers engage with the writing process differently by employing digital tools?

4. What are the benefits of collaborative writing in a digital space?

5. In reflecting on the examples provided here, how are you beginning to view writing differently with a digital space and with the aid of digital tools?

CHAPTER 9

Strategies for Building Teachers' Capacity to Make the Most of New Technologies

"If this software works, thank a teacher."
— *Classroom teacher in charge of an integrated learning system,*
interviewed by the author in 1997

In this chapter, you will learn:

- five things teachers need to know about professional development using technology;

- 10 strategies for advancing your own professional development; and

- three characteristics of schools that do a great job in supporting the professional development of teachers using technology.

After reading this chapter, you will:

- have many new strategies for using technology in your classroom;

- know how to host an Internet party;

- know how to become a fully networked teacher;

- know why you should stop worrying about what you don't know; and

- know how to become a more confident mentor as well as a more confident user of new technologies.

Professional development is vital for a teacher who wants to make good use of technology, and the good news is that, although technology and the Internet seem to change every week, the suggestions that we provide on these issues have emerged from research that has been carried out over a period of 30 years. They will remain valuable for some time to come. These suggestions are not simply our opinions—they are based on the findings of hundreds of studies into teacher change and technological development all over the world as well as the authors' work in dozens of classrooms in the United States, Ireland, and the United Kingdom.

The quotation that opens this chapter reminds us that, contrary to the views of some gurus who predicted that the Internet would spell the end of schooling, if technology is going to help learners, the teacher's role is vital. Yes, students can learn some things without the teacher's assistance, but they will learn even more if the teacher leads, encourages, and manages their learning. In a world in which students can access any one of 25 billion Internet sites with a single click, the teacher's role as a mentor, a guide, and a critical friend is not only important but it is also more significant, more substantial, and more vital than ever before.

What You Need to Know about Professional Development Using Technology

You need TPACK!

Perhaps the most important knowledge for the teacher who is using technology to have is Technological Pedagogical Content Knowledge (TPACK). There is information about TPACK elsewhere in this book as well as on the Internet, but the key insight is this: New technologies lead to new ways of teaching, most of which teachers were not taught in college, and these new approaches will only work well if all three elements—technology, content, and pedagogy—are up-to-date and integrated coherently. For example, a beginning teacher might be a very experienced user of word-processing software, but he or she might not know that the spell-checking capabilities of Microsoft Word® are often poor when dealing with the spelling of a dyslexic student. Microsoft Word® can help those whose spelling is reasonably good, but Word® 2010 doesn't offer a correct alternative to any of the four misspelled words in this sentence: *Fiziks is bootifl and it is my favrite supgekt* (Physics is beautiful and it is my favorite subject). In this case, the teacher's pedagogical content knowledge might need updating so that he or she can make a more informed decision about what software to recommend to help his or her student.

Figure 9.1 The TPACK Framework

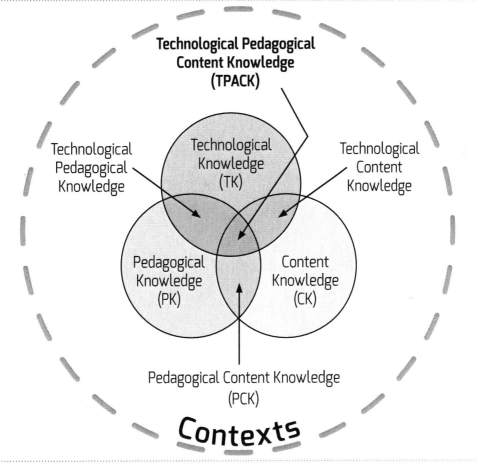

At the heart of the TPACK framework is the complex interplay of three primary forms of knowledge: Content (CK), Pedagogy (PK), and Technology (TK). For teaching to be effective, these need to be coherent, balanced, and integrated. What does it mean to have these three elements integrated coherently? Well, as the TPACK Framework diagram shows (see Figure 9.1), the three types of knowledge do not necessarily overlap, but they do need to be working together in the classroom context. An example of how this can develop is shown in the two lists in Figure 9.2, which report the changes in the use made of technology in the lessons of a teacher named Lindsay between the time she began teaching and when she was interviewed as part of the Impact 09 project in the United Kingdom (Crook et al. 2010). Lindsay was very fortunate; she was working in a school that gave her a great deal of support in becoming an expert and confident user of technologies. But while her pedagogical content knowledge was high, her technological pedigogical knowledge was initially low.

Figure 9.2 Progression as a Technology User from Beginning to Experienced

Beginning Teacher	Experienced Teacher
Lesson goals on PowerPoint®	Pre-lesson task online
"Death by PowerPoint®" exposition	Video clip to grab students' attention
Gave homework task: "Do Internet research"	Lesson goals on PowerPoint®
	Chooses PowerPoint® layout preferred by dyslexic student
	PowerPoint® to show key points of lesson
	Use of remote clicker to navigate PowerPoint®
	Prints off alternative task for one student during the lesson
	Online support for homework
	Assessment mediated by technology

Lindsay said that when she began teaching, she submitted her students to what she described as "Death by PowerPoint®." She said, "I was using [PowerPoint®] as a crutch to rely on while I was establishing myself in the school." In other words, at that stage in her career, her use of technology was driven by her need to manage her students by overloading them with information rather than by a pedagogy that coherently integrated technology, content, and learning. She asked her students to carry out homework tasks using the Internet but had not found a way of supporting them in doing this. As Figure 9.2 shows, however, as Lindsay gained an understanding of the TPACK framework, her lessons began incorporating a much wider range of technological resources, and these were much better integrated than earlier.

As a more experienced teacher, and with greater technological knowledge and technological content knowledge, Lindsay often used multimedia delivered from her computer at the start of a lesson, to grab attention and establish a topic. She then used PowerPoint® not simply to lecture but to give information that was formatted and anchored to meet her students' needs, and presented, when necessary, from any point in the classroom using her clicker, a device for remotely controlling a computer presentation.

 ## Voices from the Classroom

Use of Technology over Time

"How I use PowerPoint® has changed massively. I use a wireless clicker, so I don't have to keep walking back to the computer. It's really good because you can move forward or back to different slides from anywhere in the classroom. You can anchor the lesson around the computer, but all the time is teaching time. I use it to highlight key points...to teach new vocabulary....But I don't use it for copying any more. I hate copying. It's one of the most pointless things in the world."

Lindsay was also becoming more able to multitask within her lessons. She was able to print out a revised (and simpler) worksheet for one student while the lesson was in progress. She also had a much more long-term view of her teaching. She made it possible for her students to access a pre-lesson task online, to view feedback on their homework online, and she also provided Internet links to help those who might need extra assistance when working independently.

It is not essential to use a dozen different technologies in every lesson in order to demonstrate TPACK. In fact, most teachers agree that there will be many lessons in which a computer is an unnecessary distraction. The point here is that a teacher with a mature TPACK approach will use technology judiciously and in a manner that integrates teaching, learning, and content in a seamless and coherent way.

You Know More than You Think You Know!

Many teachers have said, "I'm not good with technology" or "I just don't do technology." But what they often mean is, "I don't feel confident when I'm using technology" or "I missed the session on how to use an electronic whiteboard, and I never caught up" or "I don't know what Web 2.0 means—in fact, I'm not sure I know very much about Web 1.0!" But many teachers whose confidence is low know much more than they think they know.

The research on teachers' confidence levels is fascinating. What researchers have found is that

- Female teachers are generally less confident about technology than male teachers.

- Male teachers are generally more confident about technology, even if they know less than female teachers.

- When they attend professional development sessions, female teachers' declared confidence levels sometimes go down as they realize how much they still want to learn.

- When they attend professional development sessions, male teachers' confidence levels often go up as they realize they have acquired new ideas. (Youngman and Harrison 1998)

So, low confidence does not necessarily imply low knowledge, and many teachers who say "I'm not good with technology" fail to give themselves credit for being highly skilled at word processing, experienced with PowerPoint®, competent at digital photography, and daily users of the Internet and a mobile phone. Sometimes, we need to remind ourselves just how far we have come since the 1980s, when a laser printer took up a whole room, a simple computer program took six minutes to load, a mobile phone cost $4,000, and the World Wide Web had not been invented.

What we do know is that teachers are happiest when they learn from people they trust—friends, partners, colleagues, and neighbors. In the early days of computers in schools (and when a laptop cost a month's salary), the UK government gave a thousand teachers a personal computer to help them become more confident in using technology in school. What the evaluators of this initiative found was that within a year, the vast majority of teachers had moved from being tentative and cautious to being expert and professional and looked for every opportunity to use their laptop in and out of school. How did this happen? The answer is that these teachers learned most from informal sources—friends, partners, colleagues, and neighbors.

In a more recent project that looked at the most successful school in England in terms of using technology to enhance school learning, it was found that teacher change had not been brought about by large-scale professional development events but by a single teacher who worked one-on-one with individuals for about an hour after school, gently advising and suggesting innovations that built upon the interests and strengths of each teacher.

Perhaps the secret to becoming more confident and more knowledgeable, therefore, is to increase significantly the number of people whom you trust to guide you, and this chapter aims to help you in this respect. Not everyone on the Internet is trustworthy, but many thousands of people are, and these people are giving up countless hours of their time in order to share their ideas with others.

So trust yourself. You are already more of an expert than you realize, and the path to becoming more of an expert can be exciting and hugely enjoyable.

Individually, Your Students Know Less than You, but Collectively, They Know More!

As teachers, we begin from an authority position. We know things that our students do not know, and we know how to help them learn those things. However, if we feel that our students are more knowledgeable than we are, we feel vulnerable. Teaching is our job, and it is our responsibility to know more than our students. But with new technologies, things have changed. We know that we have more content knowledge than our students, but we sometimes worry that they know much more than us about surfing the Internet, new media, and social media. In particular, we worry that they know much more than we do about Web 2.0.

Most kids do not know more than us. Despite the suggestion that students are now "digital natives" (Prensky 2001), while we, their teachers, are the "digital immigrants," struggling behind, trying unsuccessfully to shake off the mantle of reluctant adopters (Rogers 1976), we now know that such a construction is inaccurate. On the Internet, the 1 percent rule applies—only 1 percent of users produce and publish material, a further 10 percent go so far as to comment on what they encounter, but the other 89 percent (most of the students whom we teach) are consumers, not producers.

And there is more good news. The Impact 09 project (Crook et al. 2010) found that most of the teachers who were leaders and innovators in the use of technologies in the classroom were not geeks with a computing background; they were teachers who had learned their new approaches alongside the students they taught. This is what one teacher reported:

> *We teach one another now. I mean, you put a child on Photoshop. That software normally has five or six different ways to bring about a solution. They'll find them all. They'll teach me new ways. I'll teach them the way that I know, and they'll come up with different solutions all the time. So it's absolutely fascinating. They'll learn from me, I'll learn from them.*

Another teacher, who was able to use a digital camera, but who had no expertise in editing video, had been studying poetry with a special-needs group of 12-year-olds. She found that the one student who did have video-editing knowledge was able to teach her as well as the other students. The teacher reported:

> *I just said ... "Does anyone here know how to use (this image editing package)" and he said, "Yes, I do. I'll show you." And he taught me.... So he taught me how to do it and he taught the others.... I didn't know what I was doing. I kept saying, "What do I do now?" and he would say, "Do this and do that." And then, because he taught me, I taught [grade] 9 this year.*

There is perhaps a trend here—wider access to new technologies and to the Internet is gradually changing the authority position of teachers. These days, many students know things that we do not, and teachers are learning how to welcome this and are recruiting students as collaborators and assistants in advancing the learning of everyone in the classroom.

There Is So Much Great Material Out There—the Key Is Becoming More Skilled at Finding It!

There are tens of thousands of lesson plans, video lessons, and other educational resources out there on the Internet, many of which are of high quality and potentially engaging for your students. And you do not have to become a different kind of teacher to use them. Your teacherly personality was probably substantially formed by the age of 20. Teachers understandably resist attempts to change their approaches to teaching.

What is good about using new technologies is that it is not difficult to find material and resources that harmonize well with your own preferred tactics and strategies. Choosing the right search terms is the key. If you want to find out how to help your students do more successful group work using the Internet, there are chapters in this book to help you. But simply putting "better group work" into Google™ also sends you to authoritative and practical suggestions on how to do just that. By contrast, if you want to prepare a lecture-style presentation on the American Civil War, "civil war lecture" will give you hundreds of videos from which to choose from, ranging from a 12-lecture series from university professors to clips from television cartoons.

Teachers learn most from other teachers, and teachers who a year ago did not know what a blog was, are coming to realize that hundreds of thousands of their colleagues are now sharing ideas, plans, and resources online and are eager correspondents when contacted by a fellow professional. Most teachers' blogs are personal websites, containing opinions, information, and most importantly, resources and tips on how to use them.

Searching out the blogs of teachers who see the world the same way you do can be incredibly valuable. Not only will such teachers be offering links and fresh ideas but also others who share your values will be making their contributions to that site. A search for "iPad® apps for literacy" returns thousands of links, but the ones that come first are not commercial sites—they are mostly blogs created by groups or individuals who care about education. They have not only tried out the applications in the classroom, but they have also brought together the ideas of dozens of other teachers who have done the same. We encourage you to get out there and become a member of the blogosphere!

There Are Barriers to Overcome but Also Strategies for Overcoming Them

We know that becoming confident and an expert with new technologies is a challenge. There has been plenty of research showing that teachers can encounter problems in bringing new technologies into their classroom. Finding the time to learn about new technologies is never easy; monitoring students' use of the Internet and keeping them on task can be difficult; deciding where the privacy boundaries lie between teachers and their students can be tricky; trying to get past the school's (or the district's) Internet filters to your chosen website can be frustrating.

But schools and principals are becoming more comfortable with technology. Internet providers for schools know that the small number of students who successfully bypass Internet filters generally do so simply to engage in social networking. New rules permitting mobile phones in school, subject to strict guidelines on their use, have now been introduced replacing 10-year "no phone" policies previously held by many schools. Internet safety is a very important issue, but many schools now work with parents to spread the word about responsible behavior, to ensure the safety of everyone, including teachers.

Ten Strategies for Advancing Your Own Professional Development

In this section, we offer 10 very practical strategies for using technology to enhance your teaching. All the suggestions have been used by thousands of teachers already, but it is important to mention that flexibility is the key: an elementary classroom in El Paso is very different from a social studies class in a middle school in Spokane. So feel free to adapt these ideas to suit your own personality and your own professional setting.

Throw an Internet Party

Make your own professional development as enjoyable as possible. Throw a Web party! There isn't a fixed way to do this, but here are some possibilities:

- Host an event after school, in the most comfortable location available so that the atmosphere is relaxed and informal.

- The main goal of the event will be investigating new resources found on the Internet and sharing thoughts, plans, and adaptations with colleagues.

- Ask everyone to bring some comfort food. People learn best when they are not hungry.

- Have every participant bring a laptop or other device that can be connected to the Internet.

- At least one teacher should research, in advance, some resources to share and evaluate. Teachers might pair up to research particular media or content topics.

- Hold a video conference (that has been set up in advance) to share stories and recommendations with a different group of teachers.

- Plan a follow-up meeting in a month or so to review, report back, and critique, with everyone agreeing to take on an evaluation task.

Identify Internet Resource Banks

Set out to identify some Internet resource banks that are unfamiliar to you. Not all resources travel well across national boundaries, though differences in subjects such as history and geography can be valuable in their own right. These are just some ideas to start you off. Do not worry if you already know some of the ones listed below—there are thousands out there that you have yet to find!

- For literacy development, the International Reading Association (http://www.reading.org) has a commendably broad range of resources, including reports, podcasts from experts, and links to hundreds of lesson plans, many of which develop comprehension, critical thinking, and collaboration.

- The *Times Educational Supplement*™ (http://www.tes.co.uk) claims to anchor the largest network of teachers in the world. Membership is free (though there is a Pro membership that isn't), and the TES™ claims that its 600,000 teaching resources such as lesson plans, PowerPoint® presentations, and videos have saved the 700,000-plus teachers who use them more than half a billion hours in preparation time.

- Many teachers not only view great lessons on YouTube™ and YouTube™ Teachers but they also upload their own. Other great resources for videos of lessons are TeacherTube®, and the sadly defunct Teachers TV (whose 3,500 videos were archived and continue to be available through the TES™).

Teach Yourself New Skills

Help from colleagues or friends is ideal, but failing that, look online for assistance. There are a zillion blogs out there, but Classroom 2.0 (http://classroom2.0.com) has links to dozens of videos that show you exactly how to do some of the things you want to do, but never found out how to do, such as creating digital books, making a podcast, using Google™ Docs to create co-authored stories with your students, or using a SMART-board. A good way to begin is simply to type into the search engine search box "how to…" and your desired skill. The search term "how to use a SMART-board" generated 50,000 links last time we looked.

Make Your Students the Experts!

We all know that many students have expertise that we do not have, and one of the best ways to use and even extend that knowledge is by asking them to undertake out-of-school technology tasks that will add to your bank of resources.

- Most students have some access to a camera these days, and they can use photographs or video as part of their multimedia compositions.

- It might be worth carrying out a "skills, experience, and equipment" audit of your students to find out what they might teach you or one another.

- One teacher who despaired of engaging her students in writing had the idea of inviting them to create videos of a "Barbie Doll Olympics." There were two rules: the video had to be funny, and the video had to have a written script with a plot. As you might expect, the 11-year-old students loved the idea. They took over the teacher's idea and worked night and day on their scripts and movies, which were then filmed by the teacher, mostly in class.

Help Your Students Learn While You Sleep! (Make a Podcast)

A podcast is simply a digital file that is made available to others over the Internet. The term usually refers to an audio file (often an .mp3 or a .wav), or a video file (often an .mp4 or an .mov). Downloadable sound files of your favorite radio shows are podcasts, as are the video news bulletins from the major networks that can be accessed on smartphones. Usually podcasts created by teachers are quite short, no longer than five minutes. It turns out that students' willingness to watch a video made by a teacher generally declines after a fairly short time. But this need not be a problem—teachers can do a lot of teaching in three minutes, and in any event, video files are quite large, so files that are less than five minutes in length are preferable since they are quicker to upload and download.

Here is an exercise to help you learn more about creating a podcast.

- Go to YouTube™ and compare some of the videos that tell you about metaphor and simile. Note the professional quality of some of the videos that have had 90,000-plus views (such as that by Jane Hirshfield). Think about why some others have had less than 100 views.

- See if you can find the video defining metaphor and similes made by the Tang twins in ninth grade. It checks every box: it has music, it reflects teen culture, it has text as well as words, and it's fun!

- You don't have to take hours to make a useful podcast. See if you can find a podcast by searching for the phrase "how to use a SMART-board with VoiceThread®." There are a number of podcasts of less than a minute that give really helpful information about this topic.

- Are you ready to make a podcast? If you have a computer with a microphone and a camera, it is very straightforward. Unfortunately, most of the videos on the Internet that come up when you enter the search term "how to make a podcast" were created a few years ago, when it was much more difficult to make one. The author of this chapter just tried making a 15-second video with the Photo Booth® software on his Mac®. The icon was then dragged onto the desktop, the file was renamed, then uploaded to YouTube™, and voilà! In less than two and a half minutes, the file was uploaded and made public on the Internet.

- Go and do thou likewise! (**Tip**: You need to have a YouTube™ account in order to be able to upload a podcast, but it's free.)

Get a Clicker!

A wireless remote clicker can revolutionize how you manage the classroom from any location. As every teacher knows, being able to move around the class is a vital part of teaching. It is an important (though often a very subtle) part of classroom management since being able to move to support a student or position yourself as a member of the audience as well as the master of ceremonies can be invaluable. With a clicker, you can control your computer wirelessly from any point in the classroom. So, even if you are working with a student at the back of the class, and you discover that a crucial point has not been understood, you can go back in a presentation or even switch between applications instantly. Different clickers have slightly different controls and some have full-scrolling mouse control, but with most, you can:

- Launch/end a slide show

- Point at the screen with a laser pointer

- Go forward or back in a presentation

- Superimpose a black screen (very handy in a quiz)

- Control speaker volume

- Set a timer to warn you when your time is nearly up

Always Have a Plan B and a Plan C

Don't forget, when you are using technology, always have a Plan B (an alternative technology) and Plan C (the zero-technology option). All technologies can fail, and ultimately, all *will* fail at some point. So, it is a good idea to have Plan B and Plan C ready for emergencies. Plan B is the no-Internet plan, and Plan C is the no-electricity plan.

- Plan B: Even in a wired-up school, there can be network problems that mean you lose your Internet connection. So, Plan B would be to have some key images, Internet pages, or screenshots stored as picture files (usually .jpg format) so that if the Internet becomes unavailable, you still have some key data and images to work with.

- Plan C: Sometimes (hopefully, only rarely), the school's electricity supply is interrupted or lost. This is when you produce the paper questionnaire on technology use or ownership that you have never found time to give, or perhaps a pencil-and-paper quiz on technology use. Or you read a story!

Use Technology to Enhance Assessment

Always look for new ways to use technology to support your record keeping and assessment. Technology can be a wonderful ally in the area of assessment because all data that is transmitted is capable of being saved and thus capable of being an element in the assessment for learning process. The following are examples of some of the ways in which technology can be a significant component in formative as well as summative assessment.

- Use individual audio files to record students' developing fluency in reading aloud. Students love to come back and hear how much they've improved over (for example) six months or a year. Good organization and record keeping of file names and locations is crucial, and the teacher needs to be in charge of this.

- Audio-file recordings are not useful with just younger students. One high school teacher whom we worked with recorded his 11th-grade students' trepidation upon being asked to read and discuss *Hamlet*. Six months later, they listened to their earlier group recording and were pleased to report how much more confident they felt in dealing with Shakespeare's text.

- In 1998, our research found very few teachers who would give out their email address to students. By 2013, this was changing. We are no longer surprised to hear a teacher saying to us, "All my students have my email address, and none of them abuse or misuse it. Also, they email me drafts of their work, and I comment on them with track changes. In fact, this saves me time." The teacher who said this was not typical (in 2012), but she was one of a growing number who were using track changes to give formative feedback to students.

- Some teachers are now beginning to give students voice-memo feedback on projects. Some software even links mini-sound recordings to comment boxes on the assignment itself. What is interesting is that teachers who use this system do not see it as onerous. Some high school teachers require their students to listen to the sound file and then turn the voice memo into a bullet-point list and give them credit for doing this. Therefore, the voice memo actually saves the teacher time because the student is doing the writing up of comments.

- Another important point to remember is that students can now see one another's work over the Internet. So, there is no reason why they can't become members of the assessment community, critiquing and formatively evaluating their classmates' work. Our experience has shown that they generally do this with care and sensitivity, and for a very good reason—their classmates are going to be doing the same to them very soon!

Try to Integrate Your Technologies

A few years ago, one piece of technology was all a teacher could manage in one lesson, but this is changing. As we saw in the TPACK section above, a teacher may be using technology in a rich variety of ways. Ways that can be linked together across time and space.

- At the start of a lesson, use video clips rather than PowerPoint® in creative ways to stimulate interest but also to activate prior knowledge.

- For lesson organization and setting students' expectations, use PowerPoint® to introduce teaching and learning goals and to stimulate and encourage progression.

- When reading a work of literature, encourage multimedia responses rather than only written ones.

- For differentiation, use technology to adapt your teaching to the needs of individuals, with PowerPoint® slides in colors chosen to meet the needs of students with dyslexia and activity sheets edited and printed on the fly within a lesson to meet the needs of a struggling student.

- Use technology to encourage student-led learning. Peer assessment, collaboration, and transforming data are key pedagogic goals, and wider student choice is possible with online resources.

- Encourage student discussion via a blog. An online blog may seem unnecessary when students meet together regularly in class, but quieter students who do not participate in class discussions sometimes contribute more to an online blog. Also, students can add to their blog in their own time.

- Use technology to link school and home learning. Increasingly, teachers are learning to make the best use of the school's virtual learning environment, encouraging the students to access their online course and individual lesson plans as well as pre-lesson and post-lesson resources, both in class and from home.

Reflect on Technology in Your Teaching

Ask yourself, "How have new technologies changed my teaching?" and "What have I learned from this?" A teacher who uses technology is not necessarily a better teacher than one who does not, so it is important to reflect on how you are using technology and how you might make even better use of it. The following Pause for Thought section invites you to reflect on your own teaching using technology.

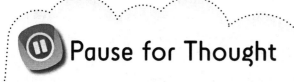

Pause for Thought

How Have New Technologies Changed My Teaching?

- Think back to your first experiences as a teacher. In what ways was technology important? How was it important for your planning and in your classroom? What technology did your students use?

- How have things changed since you began teaching? Think of the same three areas: your use of technology for planning and preparation, your use in lessons, and your students' uses of technology.

- In what areas of your teaching has technology now become indispensible?

- What have been some of the barriers to making more effective use of technology? Have these been overcome?

- What lessons have you learned about using technology that have made you a better teacher?

- Who or what has helped you most to become a more skilled user of technology?

Hopefully, answering these questions has been useful for you. Your answers to the questions above may help you to apply your learning to the questions below, which look ahead from this chapter toward your own professional development.

- Can you identify three goals that you want to achieve in extending and developing your own use of technology?

- Will you need help in achieving these goals? If so, who could help you? If you do not have an answer to this question, your best solution might be to seek help through a professional organization such as the International Reading Association or one of its national affiliates.

Characteristics of Schools That Support the Professional Development of Teachers Using Technology

Research has shown that schools vary enormously in how well they support the professional development of teachers, and there can also be wide disparities in how effectively different schools support the use of technology. As researchers, the authors of this book have visited schools that have detailed and lengthy policy documents that set out ambitious goals for developing the use of technology for learning, but the use of technology for learning is only apparent in one or two classrooms in the whole school. On the other hand, we have been to schools that have a policy for extending the uses of technology for learning that is only half a page in length, but every classroom, every teacher, and every student is buzzing with the excitement of transforming learning through technology. The schools in which technology is thriving, and in which the teachers feel empowered and confident in using technology, share three features:

- **The school possesses leadership that has vision,** provides sustainable resources for learning, and supports teachers' professional development in ways that are encouraging but not threatening.

- **There is technical support** for teachers that provides rapid and effective assistance when problems arise, whether they relate to infrastructure ("Why is it taking 15 minutes of my lesson for 16 computers to log in to the school network?") or to software ("Why doesn't the data projector display on the big screen a PowerPoint® picture that is on my laptop?").

- **Teachers are encouraged to innovate**, and there is a culture that provides time for this and reassures them that small steps forward are fine. Every colleague is involved in a collaborative process.

Building communities of learners is not easy, and it isn't any easier to build a community of learning teachers than a community of learning students. But if the goal is to build a community of teachers who are learning about better ways to use technology to develop their professional practice, there are a number of ways in which this is easier than it used to be. First, nearly all teachers are in fact already experts in using technology—a laptop, a phone, surfing the Internet, and all the mini-computers with which we manage our domestic lives. Second, many teachers are already good at using technology to communicate within various groups—family members, colleagues, basketball moms, and so on. Third, the students of those teachers are experts not only in using technology but also in using it to form and sustain groups and small communities. Extending these skills into the arena of professional development around the topic of technology for learning is therefore not only possible but also relatively easy and exciting, and it can be hugely enjoyable and satisfying.

Final Words: Why Should We Be Using Technology in Our Teaching?

Strangely, educators have not always thought deeply about *why* we should use more technology in our teaching. Governments tend to believe that a technological education is vital to developing employability skills and life skills. But is this the case? And even if it is, as educators, do we accept this argument? As a coda to this very practical book, it is perhaps worth at least briefly addressing this question.

We want to suggest that since the 1980s, there have been two main belief systems that have driven the introduction of computers in schools, and that more recently a third rationale has emerged. The first belief system that provided a rationale for using new technologies was associated with motivation—a belief that since computers in school enhanced motivation, they would also enhance learning. Well, early research suggested that computers did increase motivation and this is still largely the case, but there was much less evidence available on the impact of technology on learning. The second set of beliefs grew as the Internet came into schools—computers were important because they would revolutionize communication. This philosophy had some moral depth, and it was associated with some imaginative international educational initiatives, but many of these approaches became compromised in the struggle to ensure students' Internet safety at home and at school, and communication between schools (for example, using email) is now actively discouraged in many countries. In many respects, the third-belief system, which we might call "four-dimensional (4-D) learning," is not new, but it is important.

The concept of 4-D learning (learning anywhere, at any time) is associated with the themes of ubiquitous (anytime, anywhere) computing, of collaborative learning, and of production rather than consumption of media texts. These principles have been on many people's agenda in the technology field for over a decade, but many in education are only just beginning to put the goal of participation across space and time at the top of the agenda and to recognize that this is a goal that can transform the nature of education and lead to students accomplishing within a school environment many of the goals that Roger Schank argued (1994, 2002) could only be achieved by dismantling schools.

So what happens when a school takes on this belief system and moves toward 4-D learning? Again, research provides some answers. This is how Stephenson School revised its goals. The teachers, guided and led by a visionary management team, agreed on the following priorities:

- Put the focus on improving learning

- Understand that 24/7 access to learning is essential for students and teachers

- Develop ways to better merge learning and assessment

- Revise the concept of who is a teacher and who is a learner

- Explore opportunities to make learners into producers rather than consumers

It was by following those steps that the teachers at Stephenson School transformed learning for their students and became not only excited but professionally renewed. As the art teacher put it, "Kids from a working-class area [of a town in the North of England] have got an international forum now for their work, and isn't that just fantastically exciting?...And you couldn't do that without technology." (Teacher interview, Stephenson School; November 3, 2009.)

Questions for Reflection

1. In what ways has your use of technology for preparing lessons and in delivering lessons changed over the past year?

2. What plans for future uses of technology do you have in place?

3. Do you believe that "anytime, anywhere learning" has already begun to impact the students with whom you work? If so, in what ways? What are the implications for you as a teacher?

4. Which of the following have impacted your teaching this year? Explain the impact they have had on your teaching.

   • Ideas from friends, or colleagues in your own workplace
   • Ideas from people you've met at conferences or professional development events
   • Ideas from Internet sources (e.g., blogs, videos of teaching, lesson plan template)
   • Ideas from this book

References Cited

Agosto, Denise E. 2002. "Bounded Rationality and Satisficing in Young People's Web-Based Decision-Making." *Journal of the American Society for Information Science and Technology* 53: 16–27.

Allington, Richard L. 1983. "The Reading Instruction Provided Readers of Differing Reading Abilities." *The Elementary School Journal* 83 (5): 548–559.

Allington, Richard L. 2001. *What Really Matters for Struggling Readers: Designing Research-Based Programs.* New York: Longman.

Anderson, Richard C., and William E. Nagy. 1992. "The Vocabulary Conundrum." *American Educator* 16 (4): 14–18, 44–47.

Armbruster, Bonnie B., and Thomas H. Anderson. 1984. "Producing 'Considerate' Expository Text: Or Easy Reading Is Damned Hard Writing." *Reading Education Report* 46. University of Illinois at Urbana-Champaign: Center for the Study of Reading.

Barron, Brigid. 2003. "When Smart Groups Fail." *Journal of the Learning Sciences* 12 (3): 307–359.

Beck, Isabel L., Margaret G. McKeown, and Linda Kucan. 2002. *Bringing Words to Life: Robust Vocabulary Instruction.* New York: Guilford Press.

Bennett, Sue, Karl Matton, and Lisa Kervin. 2008. "The 'Digital Natives' Debate: A Critical Review of the Evidence." *British Journal of Educational Technology* 39 (5): 775–786.

Biancarosa, Gina, and Catherine Snow. 2006. *Reading Next: A Vision for Action and Research in Middle and High School Literacy: A Report to Carnegie Corporation of New York.* Washington, DC: Alliance for Excellent Education. 2nd edition.

Bilal, Dania. 2000. "Children's Use of the Yahooligans! Web Search Engine: I. Cognitive, Physical, and Affective Behaviors on Fact-Based Search Tasks." *Journal of the American Society for Information Science* 51 (7): 646–665.

Birkerts, Sven. 1994. *The Gutenberg Elegies: The Fate of Reading in an Electronic Age.* Boston: Faber and Faber.

Blachowicz, Camille L. Z., and Peter Fisher. 2004. "Keep the 'Fun' in Fundamental: Encouraging Word Awareness and Incidental Word Learning in the Classroom Through Word Play." In *Vocabulary Instruction: Research to Practice*, edited by Edward J. Kame'enui and James F. Baumann, 218–237. New York: Guilford Press.

Block, Cathy Collins, and Michael Pressley, eds. 2002. *Comprehension Instruction: Research-Based Best Practices.* New York: Guilford Press.

Boling, Erica, Jill Castek, Lisa Zawilinski, Karen Barton, and Theresa Nierlich. 2008. "Collaborative Literacy: Blogs and Internet Projects." *The Reading Teacher* 61: 504–506.

Boyne, John. 2006. *The Boy in the Striped Pajamas.* London: Random House.

Brown, Ronan, Rob Waring, and Sangrawee Donkaewbua. 2008. "Incidental Vocabulary Acquisition from Reading, Reading-While-Listening, and Listening." *Reading in a Foreign Language* 20: 136–163.

Burke, Jim. 2002. "The Internet Reader." *Educational Leadership* 60 (3): 38–42.

Castek, Jill M. 2008. "How Do 4th and 5th Grade Students Acquire the New Literacies of Online Reading Comprehension? Exploring the Contexts that Facilitate Learning" (PhD diss., University of Connecticut).

Castek, Jill, Julie Coiro, Lizbeth Guzniczak, and Carlton Bradshaw. 2012. "Examining Peer Collaboration in Online Inquiry." *The Educational Forum* 76: 479–496.

Castek, Jill, Bridget Dalton, and Dana Grisham. 2012. "Using Multimedia to Support Students' Generative Vocabulary Learning." In *Vocabulary Instruction: Research to Practice*, 2nd edition, edited by James F. Baumann and Edward J. Kame'enui. New York, NY: Guilford Press.

Castek, Jill, and Jen Tilson. 2012. "Using iPad Apps to Extend Literacy and Content Learning." Paper presented at the International Reading Association Conference (IRA) Pre-Conference Institute: *Fostering Literacy with Research Based Instructional Practices and Web 2.0 Technologies*, Chicago, IL.

Coiro, Julie, Jill Castek, and Lizbeth Guzniczak. 2011. "Uncovering Online Reading Comprehension Processes: Two Adolescents Reading Independently and Collaboratively on the Internet." In *60th Annual Yearbook of the Literacy Research Association*, edited by Pamela Dunston, Linda B. Gambrell, Kathy Headley, Susan King Fullerton, Pamela M. Stecker, Vanessa R. Gillis, and C. C. Bates, 354–369. Oak Creek, WI: Literacy Research Association.

Common Core State Standards. 2010. *Common Core State Standards for English Language Arts and Literacy in History/Social Studies, Science, and Technical Subjects*. Washington, DC: National Governors Association.

Crawford, James. 2004. *Educating English Learners: Language Diversity in the Classroom*, 5th edition. Los Angeles, CA: Bilingual Education Services, Inc.

Crook, Charles, and Colin Harrison. 2008. "Web 2.0 Technologies for Learning at Key Stage 3 and 4: Summary Report." Coventry, UK: British Educational Communications and Technology Agency (BECTA).

Crook, Charles, Colin Harrison, Lee Farrington-Flint, Carmen Tomás, and Jean Underwood. 2010. *The Impact of Technology: Value-Added Classroom Practice.* Coventry, UK: British Educational Communications and Technology Agency (BECTA).

Dalton, Bridget. 2008. "Integrating Language, Culture, and Technology to Achieve New Literacies for All." In *Technology-Mediated Learning Environments for Young English Learners,* edited by L. Leann Parker. New York: Lawrence Erlbaum Associates.

Dalton, Bridget, and C. Patrick Proctor. 2008. "The Changing Landscape of Text and Comprehension in the Age of the New Literacies." In *Handbook of Research on New Literacies,* edited by Julie Coiro, Michele Knobel, Colin Lankshear, and Donald J. Leu, 297–324. Mahwah, NJ: Lawrence Erlbaum Associates.

Dalton, Bridget, and Nicole Strangman. 2006. "Improving Struggling Readers' Comprehension Through Scaffolded Hypertexts and Other Computer-Based Literacy Programs." In *International Handbook of Literacy and Technology: Volume 11,* edited by Michael C. McKenna, Linda D. Labbo, Ronald D. Kieffer, and David Reinking, 75–92. Mahwah, NJ: Lawrence Erlbaum Associates.

Daniels, Harvey. 2002. *Literature Circles: Voice and Choice in Book Clubs and Reading Groups.* Portland, Maine: Stenhouse.

Davey, Beth. 1983. "Think Aloud: Modeling the Cognitive Process of Reading Comprehension." *Journal of Reading* 27 (1): 44–47.

de Lotbinière, Max. 2010. "Language Reaches Poor by Mobile Phone." London: *The Guardian.* Accessed January 2011. http://www.guardian .co.uk/education/2010/dec/07/language-lesson-mobile-phones-lotbiniere.

DeSchryver, Mike, and Randi Spiro. 2008. "New Forms of Deep Learning on The Web: Meeting the Challenge of Cognitive Load in Conditions of Unfettered Exploration in Online Multimedia Environments." In *Cognitive Effects of Multimedia Environments,* edited by Robert Zheng, 134–152. Hershey, PA: IGI Global.

DiCamillo, Kate. 2006. *The Miraculous Journey of Edward Tulane.* Somersville, MA: Candlewick Press.

Dobler, Elizabeth. 2013. "Letter to the Reader Beware: Evaluating Digital Books." *Literacy Beat Blog.* Retrieved from http://literacybeat.com/2013/01/30/let-the-reader-beware-evaluating-digital-books/.

Dole, Janice A., Gerald G. Duffy, Laura R. Roehler, and P. David Pearson. 1991. "Moving from the Old to the New: Research on Reading Comprehension Instruction." *Review of Educational Research* 61 (2): 239–264.

Dr. Seuss. 1978. *I Can Read with My Eyes Shut.* New York: Random House Inc.

Duke, Nell K., and P. David Pearson. 2002. "Effective Practices for Developing Reading Comprehension." In *What Research Has to Say About Reading Instruction*, 3rd edition, edited by Alan E. Farstrup and S. Jay Samuels, 205-264. Newark, DE: International Reading Association.

Dwyer, Bernadette. 2010. "Scaffolding Internet Reading: A Study of a Disadvantaged School Community in Ireland" (PhD diss., University of Nottingham, UK).

Dwyer, Bernadette, and Lotta Larson. 2014. "The Writer in the Reader: Building Communities of Response in Digital Environments." In *Exploring Technology for Writing and Writing Instruction*, edited by Kristine E. Pytash and Richard E. Ferdig, 202–220. Hersey, PA: IGI Global Publications.

Eagleton, M. B. 2005. "Factors That Influence the Internet Inquiry Process: A Cueing System Analysis of Web-Based Texts." Paper presented at the 55th Annual Meeting of the National Reading Conference, Miami, Florida.

Eagleton, Maya B., and Dobler, Elizabeth. 2007. *Reading the Web: Strategies for Internet Inquiry.* New York: Guildford.

Ferguson, Christopher J., Claudia San Miguel, Adolfo Garza, and Jessica M. Jerabeck. 2012. "A Longitudinal Test of Video Game Violence Influences on Dating and Aggression: A 3-Year Longitudinal Study of Adolescents." *Journal of Psychiatric Research* 46, 141–146.

Fogg, B. J., Jonathan Marshall, Othman Laraki, Alex Osipovich, Chris Varma, Nicholas Fang, Jyoti Paul, Akshay Rangnekar, John Shon, Preeti Swani, and Marissa Treinen. 2001. "What Makes a Website Credible? A Report on a Large Quantitative Study." Presented at the Computer-Human Interaction Conference, Seattle, Washington.

Friedman, Thomas L. 2005. *The World Is Flat. The Globalized World in the Twenty-First Century.* London: Penguin Books Ltd.

Gambrell, Linda B. 1996. "Creating Classroom Cultures That Foster Reading Motivation." *The Reading Teacher* 50: 14–25.

Gee, James Paul. 2003. *What Video Games Have to Teach Us About Learning and Literacy.* New York: Palgrave Macmillan.

Gee, James Paul. 2005. "Learning by Design: Good Video Games as Learning Machines." *E-Learning* 2 (1): 5–16.

Gee, James Paul. 2008. *Getting Over the Slump: Innovation Strategies to Promote Students's Learning.* New York: The Joan Ganz Cooney Center at Sesame Workshop.

Graves, Michael F. 2006. *The Vocabulary Book: Learning and Instruction.* New York; Newark, DE; and Urbana, IL: Teachers College Press.

Guthrie, John T. 2004. "Classroom Contexts for Engaged Reading: An Overview." In *Motivating Reading Comprehension: Concept-Oriented Reading Instruction,* edited by John T. Guthrie, Allan Wigfield, and Kathleen C. Perencevich, 87–112. Mahwah, NJ: Lawrence Erlbaum Associates.

Guthrie, John T., and Allan Wigfield. 2000. Engagement and Motivation in Reading. In *Handbook of Reading Research: Volume* III, edited by Michael L. Kamil, Peter B. Mosenthal, P. David Pearson, and Rebecca Barr, 403–422. New York: Lawrence Erlbaum Associates.

Hall, Tracey, Nicole Strangman, and Anne Meyer. 2003. "Differentiated Instruction and Implications for UDL Implementation." Wakefield, MA: National Center on Accessing the General Curriculum. Retrieved August 7, 2012. http://aim.cast.org/learn/historyarchive/ backgroundpapers/differentiated_instruction_vol.1Ut6k7hpTmm8

Harrison, Colin. 2011. "Literacy, Technology and the Internet: What Are the Challenges and Opportunities for Learners with Reading Difficulties, and How Do We Support Them in Meeting Those Challenges and Grasping Those Opportunities?" In *Multiple Perspectives on Difficulties in Learning Literacy and Numeracy*, edited by Claire Wyatt-Smith, John Elkins, and Stephanie Gunn, 111–132. New York, NY: Springer.

Harrison, Colin, Mick Youngman, Mary Bailey, Tony Fisher, Richard Phillips, and Jane Restorick. 1998. *Multimedia Portables for Teachers Pilot: Project Report.* Coventry, UK: BECTA.

Hertzberg, M. 2012. *Teaching English Language Learners in Mainstream Classes.* Australia: Primary English Teaching Association.

International Reading Association. 2009. "New Literacies and 21st Century Technologies: A Position Statement." Newark, DE: IRA. Retrieved February 1, 2010, from www.reading.org/General/AboutIRA /PositionStatements/21stCenturyLiteracies.aspx.

Ito, Mizuko, Sonja Baumer, Matteo Bittanti, Danah Boyd, Rachel Cody, Becky Herr-Stephenson, Heather A. Horst, Patricia G. Lange, Dilan Mahendran, Katynka Z. Martinez, C. J. Pascoe, Dan Perkel, Laura Robinson, Christo Sims, and Lisa Trip. 2010. *Hanging Out, Messing Around, and Geeking Out: Kids Living and Learning with New Media.* Cambridge, MA: MIT Press.

Johnson, David W., and Roger T. Johnson. 1999. "Making Cooperative Learning Work." *Theory into Practice* 38 (2): 67–73.

Kerr, Norbert L., and Steven E. Bruun. 1983. "Dispensability of Member Effort and Group Motivation Losses: Free Rider Effects." *Journal of Personality and Social Psychology* 44 (1): 78–94.

Kucan, Linda, and Isabel L. Beck. 1997. "Thinking Aloud and Reading Comprehension Research: Inquiry, Instruction and Social Interaction." *Review of Educational Research* 67 (3): 271–279.

Kuiper, Els, and Monique Volman. 2008. "The Web as a Source of Information for K–12 Education." In *Handbook of Research on New Literacies*, edited by Julie Coiro, Michele Knobel, Colin Lankshear, and Donald J. Leu, 267-296. Mahwah, NJ: Lawrence Erlbaum Associates.

Labbo, Linda D., A. Jonathan Eakle, and M. Kristiina Montero. 2002. "Digital Language Experience Approach: Using Digital Photographs and Software as a Language Experience Approach Innovation." *Reading Online* 5 (8).

LaBerge, David, and S. Jay Samuels. 1974. "Toward a Theory of Automatic Information Processing in Reading." *Cognitive Psychology* 6: 293–323.

Lankshear, Colin, and Michele Knobel. 2001. "Do We Have Your Attention? New Literacies, Digital Technologies and the Education of Adolescents." In *New Literacies and Digital Technologies: A Focus on Adolescent Learners*, edited by Donna E. Alvermann. New York: Peter Lang.

Larson, Lotta C. 2009. "e-Reading and e-Responding: New Tools for the Next Generation of Readers." *Journal of Adolescent and Adult Literacy* 53 (3): 255– 258.

Lenhart, A., M. Madden, A. Smith, and A. Magille. 2007. "Teens and Social Media." Pew Internet and American Life Project. Retrieved from http://www.pewinternet.org/Reports/2007/Teens-and-Social-Media.aspx .

Leu, Donald J. 1997. "Caity's Question: Literacy as Deixis on the Internet." *The Reading Teacher* 51: 62–67.

Leu, Donald J. 2002. "The New Literacies: Research on Reading Instruction With the Internet and Other Digital Technologies." In *What Research Has to Say About Reading Instruction*, edited by Alan E. Farstrup and S. Jay Samuels, 310–336. Newark, DE: International Reading Association.

Leu, Donald J., Julie Coiro, Jill Castek, Douglas K. Hartman, Laurie A. Henry, and David Reinking. 2008. "Research on Instruction and Assessment in the New Literacies of Online Reading Comprehension." In *Comprehension Instruction: Research-Based Best Practices*, 2nd edition, edited by Cathy Collins Block and Sheri R. Parris, 321-346. New York: The Guildford Press.

Lorenzon, Michael. 2002. "The Land of Confusion? High School Students and Their Use of the World Wide Web for Research." *Research Strategies* 18 (12): 151-163.

McKeown, Margaret G., and Isabel L. Beck. 2004. "Direct and Rich Vocabulary Instruction." In *Vocabulary Instruction: Research to Practice*, edited by James F. Baumann and Edward J. Kame'enui, 13–27. New York: Guilford Press.

McLaughlin, Maureen, and Mary Beth Allen. 2002. *Guided Comprehension: A Teaching Model for Grades 3–8*. Newark, DE: International Reading Association.

Metzger, Miriam J. 2007. "Making Sense of Credibility on the Web: Models for Evaluating Online Information and Recommendations for Future Research." *Journal of the American Society for Information Science and Technology* 58 (13): 2078–2091.

Mishra, Punya, and Matthew J. Koehler. 2006. "Technological Pedagogical Content Knowledge: A New Framework for Teacher Knowledge." *Teachers College Record* 108 (6): 1017–1054.

Nagy, William E., and Judith A. Scott. 2000. "Vocabulary Processes." In *Handbook of Reading Research: Volume* III, edited by Michael L. Kamil, Peter B. Mosenthal, P. David Pearson, and Rebecca Barr, 269–294. New York: Longman.

National Governors Association Center for Best Practices (NGA Center) and the Council of Chief State School Officers (CCSSO). 2012. Common Core State Standards Initiative. Accessed July 2. http://www.corestandards.org.

National Governors Association Center for Best Practices and Council of Chief State School Officers. 2010. *Common Core State Standards for English Language Arts and Literacy in History/Social Studies, Science, and Technical Subjects.* Washington, DC: Authors.

National Institute of Child Health and Human Development (NICHHD). 2000. *Report of the National Reading Panel. Teaching Children to Read: An Evidence-Based Assessment of the Scientific Research Literature on Reading and its Implications for Reading Instruction,* Reports of the subgroups. NIH Publication No. 00–4769. Washington, DC: U.S. Government Printing Office.

O'Brien, David, and Cassandra Scharber. 2008. "Digital Literacies Go to School: Potholes and Possibilities." *Journal of Adolescent and Adult Literacy* 52 (1): 66–68.

Ogle, Donna M. 1986. "K-W-L: A Teaching Model That Develops Active Reading of Expository Text." *The Reading Teacher* 39 (6): 564–570.

Owens, Roxanne Farwick, Jennifer L. Hester, and William H. Teale. 2002. "Where Do You Want to Go Today? Inquiry-Based Learning and Technology Integration." *The Reading Teacher* 55 (7): 616–625.

Palincsar, Annemarie Sullivan, and Ann L. Brown. 1984. "Reciprocal Teaching of Comprehension-Fostering and Comprehension-Monitoring Activities." *Cognition and Instruction* 1 (2): 117–175.

Partnership for 21st Century Learning Skills. 2007. "Framework for 21st Century Learning." Retrieved from http://www.21stcenturyskills.org.

Paton, Graeme. 2009. "Internet and Mobile Phones are 'Damaging Education'." London: *The Telegraph.* Accessed January 2011. http://www.telegraph.co.uk/education/6163309/Internet-and-mobile-phones-are-damaging -education.html.

Pearson, P. David. 2006. "Effective Comprehension Assessment in Grades 2–5." Paper presented at the annual meeting of the American Education Research Association, Los Angeles, CA.

Pearson, P. David, and Margaret C. Gallagher. 1983. "The Instruction of Reading Comprehension." *Contemporary Educational Psychology* 8: 317–344.

Pikulski, John J., and David J. Chard. 2005. "Fluency: Bridge Between Decoding and Reading Comprehension." *The Reading Teacher* 58: 510–519.

Prensky, Marc. 2001. "Digital Natives, Digital Immigrants." *On the Horizon* 9 (5): 1–6. Accessed July 9, 2012. http://www.scribd.com/doc/9799 /Prensky-Digital-Natives-Digital-Immigrants-Part1.

Pressley, Michael, and Peter Afflerbach. 1995. *Verbal Protocols for Reading: The Nature of Constructively Responsive Reading.* Hillsdale, NJ: Lawrence Erlbaum Associates.

Putney, LeAnn G., Judith Green, Carol Dixon, Richard Durán, and Beth Yeager. 2000. "Consequential Progressions: Exploring Collective-Individual Development in a Bilingual Classroom." In *Vygotskian Perspectives on Literacy Research: Constructing Meaning Through Collaborative Inquiry*, edited by Carol D. Lee and Peter Smagorinsky, 86–126. New York: Cambridge University Press.

RAND Reading Study Group. 2002. *Reading for Understanding: Toward an R&D Program in Reading Comprehension.* Santa Monica, CA: RAND.

Raphael, Taffy E., Susan Florio-Ruane, and MariAnne George. 2001. "Book Club 'Plus': A Conceptual Framework to Organize Literacy Instruction." *Language Arts* 79 (2): 159–168.

Rasinski, Timothy V. 1990. "Effects of Repeated Reading and Listening-While-Reading on Reading Fluency." *Journal of Educational Research* 83 (3): 147–150.

Rasinski, Timothy V., and S. Jay Samuels. 2011. "Reading Fluency: What It Is and What It Is Not." In *What Research Has to Say About Reading Instruction*, 4th ed., 94–114. Newark, DE: International Reading Association.

Rideout, Victorica J., Ulla G. Foehr, and D. F. Roberts. 2010. *Generation M2: Media in the Lives of 8- to 18-Year Olds.* Menlo Park, CA: Henry J. Kaiser Family Foundation.

Rogers, Everett M. 1976. "New Product Adoption and Diffusion." *The Journal of Consumer Research* 2 (4): 290–301.

Rose, David H., and Anne Meyer. 2002. *Teaching Every Student in the Digital Age: Universal Design for Learning.* Alexandria, VA: Association for Supervision and Curriculum Development.

Ryan, Aileen. 2012. "An Exploration into How Digital Texts Can Enhance the Language Experience Approach in a DEIS School" (master's thesis, Dublin City University, Ireland).

Schacter, John, Gregory K. W. K. Chung, and Aimée Dorr. 1998. "Children's Internet Searching on Complex Problems: Performance and Process Analyses." *Journal of the American Society for Information Science* 49 (9): 840–849.

Schank, R. 1994. "Top Ten Mistakes in Education." Available at http://www.engines4ed.org/hyperbook/nodes/node-283-pg.html. Accessed January 20, 2014.

Schank, R. 2002. "Are We Going to Get Smarter?" NCET Multimedia Portables for Teachers Evaluation Report. Coventry, UK: NCET.

Schiefele, Ulrich. 1999. "Interest and Learning from Text." *Scientific Studies of Reading* 3 (3): 257–279.

Scott, Judith A., and William E. Nagy. 2004. "Developing Word Consciousness." In *Vocabulary Instruction: Research to Practice*, edited by James F. Baumann and Edward J. Kame'enui, 201–217. New York: Guilford Press.

Smith, Robert Paul. 1957, 2010. *Where Did You Go? Out. What Did You Do? Nothing.* New York: W. W. Norton.

Sutherland-Smith, Wendy. 2002. "Weaving the Literacy Web: Changes in Reading From Page to Screen." *The Reading Teacher* 55 (7): 662–669.

Teale, William H., and Linda B. Gambrell. 2007. "Raising Urban Students' Literacy Achievement by Engaging in Authentic, Challenging Work." *The Reading Teacher* 60 (8): 728–739.

Tierney, Robert J. 2000. "Literacy Assessment Reform: Shifting Beliefs, Principled Possibilities, and Emerging Practices." In *Distinguished Educators on Reading: Contributions That Have Shaped Effective Literacy Instruction*, edited by Nancy D. Padak et al., 517–541. Newark, DE: International Reading Association.

Turner, Julianne, and Scott G. Paris. 1995. "How Literacy Tasks Influence Students's Motivation for Literacy." *The Reading Teacher* 48 (8), 662–675.

University College London CIBER Group. 2008. *Information Behaviour of the Researcher of the Future*. London: University College London. Accessed September 2. http://www.bl.uk/news/pdf/googlegen.pdf.

Vygotsky, Lev S. 1978. *Mind in Society: The Development of Higher Psychological Processes*. Cambridge, MA: Harvard University Press.

White, E. B. 1952. *Charlotte's Web*. London: Puffin Books.

Youngman, Mick B., and Colin Harrison. 1998. NCET Multimedia Portables for Teachers Evaluation Report. Coventry, UK: NCET.

Zawilinski, Lisa. 2009. "HOT Blogging: A Framework for Blogging to Promote Higher Order Thinking." *The Reading Teacher* 62 (8): 650–661.

Recommended URLs

Chapter 2

Runescape
http://www.runescape.com

Wiki
http://www.pbworks.com

Chapter 3

Wordle™
http://www.wordle.net

Tagxedo
http://www.tagxedo.com

Google Docs™
http://docs.google.com

Titan Pad
http://titanpad.com/ref

WordSift
http://www.wordsift.com

Literacy Beat Blog
http://literacybeat.com/2011/05/03/vocabvid-stories-developing
-vocabulary-depth-and-breadth-through-live-action-video/.

WordSift Demonstration Video on YouTube
http://www.youtube.com/watch?v=Ralb_GNs_U8

Scientifically Speaking Movie by Nick Mitchell and Katrina Theilman
http://vimeo.com/42777257

Vocabahead™
http://www.vocabahead.com

Bridget Dalton's YouTube™ Vocab Video
http://www.youtube.com/watch?v=Mq6lKJkJEmsandfeatur

ShowMe
http://www.showme.com

ShowMe Student-Created Examples
http://www.showme.com/sh/?h=hr1KoWe

ShowMe Multiple Meaning Words
http://www.showme.com/search/?q=multiple+meaning+words

VoiceThread®
http://ed.voicethread.com

VoiceThread® Instructions
http://educationalsoftware.wikispaces.com/file/view/VoiceThread.pdf

VoiceThread® Online Tutorials
http://voicethread.com/#c28

VoiceThread4education®
http://voicethread4education.wikispaces.com

Doppelme
http://doppelme.com

Thinglink Donna Baumach Example
http://auntytechideas.tumblr.com

Photovisi
http://www.photovisi.com

Podbean
http://www.podbean.com

Audacity®
http://audacity.sourceforge.net

Garage Band®
http://www.apple.com/mac/garageband

Readers Theatre
http://www.readinglady.com
http://www.aaronshep.com/rt/index.html
http://www.readingonline.org/electronic/elec_index.asp?HREF=carrick/index.html
http://www.timelessteacherstuff.com

Explor-eBooks
http://www.teachercreatedmaterials.com/apps/current/explor_ebook

Project Gutenberg
http://www.gutenberg.org/wiki/Main_Page

Storyline Online
http://www.storylineonline.net

Tumblebooks™
http://www.tumblebooks.com/library/asp/about.asp

The International Children's Digital Library
http://en.childrenslibrary.org

Monterey Bay Aquarium Pup's Supper/La Cena del Cachorro
http://www.montereybayaquarium.org/media/pups_supper/pups_supper.html

NASA's Sun-Earth Day Multimedia Students' Books
http://sunearthday.nasa.gov/2006/multimedia/books.php

The Rainforest Alliance Virtual Story Books
http://www.rainforest-alliance.org/kids/stories

Book Builder
http://bookbuilder.cast.org

Chapter 4

Monterey Bay Aquarium Foundation

http://www.montereybayaquarium.org/media/pups_supper/pups_supper.html

Sea Otter Challenge

http://www.aquariumofpacific.org/flash/otters/index.htm

Literacy Beat Blog (Beth's Dobler)

http://literacybeat.com/2013/01/30/let-the-reader-beware-evaluating-digital-books

Unite for Literacy

http://uniteforlitearacy.com

Digital Book Evaluation Rubric

https://docs.google.com/document/d/1dwp9ChmyAGupox6osbOpOidqnHLjJlyLJ7h2310pQpQ/edit

e-Book Reading and Response: Innovative Ways to Engage with Texts

http://www.readwritethink.org/classroom-resources/lesson-plans/book-reading-response-innovative-30670.html

Thoughtful Threads: Sparking Rich Online Discussions

http://www.readwritethink.org/classroom-resources/lesson-plans/thoughtful-threads-sparking-rich-1165.html

iBooks®

http://www.apple.com/ibooks-author

Chapter 5

Yahooligans™

http://www.squirrelnet.com

Screencast-o-matic

http://www.screencast-o-matic.com

Camtasia®

http://www.techsmith.com

Jing®

http://www.techsmith.com/jing.html

Webspiration®
http://www.mywebspiration.com

Popplet
http://popplet.com

Bubbl.us
http://bubbl.us

CmapTools®
http://cmap.ihmc.us

Creately™
http://creately.com

Padlet
http://padlet.com

Stormboard
http://stormboard.com

NoteApp
http://noteapp.com

Diigo®
http://www.diigo.com

Edmodo
http://www.edmodo.com/home

askkids™
http://www.askkids.com

quinturakids™
http://quinturakids.com

Google Scholar™
http://scholar.google.com

Yahoo™
http://ie.yahoo.com/?p=us

ipl2
http://www.ipl.org

Zuula™

http://www.zuula.com

Dogpile®

http://www.dogpile.com

Meta Crawler®

http://www.metacrawler.com

Yippy®

http://yippy.com

Picsearch™

http://www.picsearch.com

Truveo

http://www.truveo.com

Instagrok

http://www.instagrok.com

Twurdy

http://www.twurdy.com

Noodle Tools®

http://www.noodletools.com/debbie/literacies/information/5locate/adviceengine.html

Noodle Quest®

http://www.noodletools.com/noodlequest

Save the Pacific Northwest Trees Octopus

http://zapatopi.net/treeoctopus

Customized Google™ Search Engine

http://www.google.ie/edu/resources/custom-search-engine.html

SnappyWords

http://www.snappywords.com

WordNet®

http://wordnet.princeton.edu

Visual Thesaurus®

http://visualthesaurus.com

Visuwords™
http://visuwords.com

Teoma®
http://www.Teoma.com

Unpacking the Elements Within a URL
http://kids.nationalgeographic.com/kids/animals

Chapter 6

Missouri Botanical Gardens/Evergreen Project
http://www.readwritethink.org/classroom-resources/lesson-plans/traveling-terrain-comprehending-nonfiction-98.html

BrowseAloud
http://www.browsealoud.com

Instagrok
http://www.instagrok.com

Readability Plus
http://www.micropowerandlight.com/rd.html

Yolink®
http://www.yolink.com

Yolink Educational Site®
http://www.yolinkeducation.com

Diigo®
http://www.diigo.com

Dr. Martin Luther King Jr.
http://www.thekingcenter.org

The Good, the Bad, and the Ugly
http://lib.nmsu.edu/instruction/eval.html

Kathy Schrock's Guide for Educators
http://www.schrockguide.net/critical-evaluation.html

21st Century Information Fluency Project
http://21cif.com/tools

Internet Detective

http://www.vts.intute.ac.uk/detective

Criteria for Evaluation of Internet Information Resources

http://www.vuw.ac.nz/staff/alastair_smith/evaln/index.html

RADCAB™

http://www.radcab.com

University of Maryland University College

http://www.umuc.edu/library/libhow/websearching.cfm

Inspiration®

http://www.inspiration.com

Kidspiration®

http://www.inspiration.com/Kidspiration

Exploratree

http://www.exploratree.org.uk

ReadWriteThink Website

http://www.readwritethink.org

International Reading Association

http://www.reading.org

ReadWriteThink Summarizing Lesson

http://www.readwritethink.org/classroom-resources/lesson-plans/guided-comprehension-summarizing-using-231.html?tab=4#tabs

Chapter 7

Google docs™

http://docs.google.com

Ning

http://www.ning.com

Wiki Spaces

http://www.wiki.com

California's Velcro Crop Under Challenge

http://www.umbachconsulting.com/miscellany/velcro.html

Snopes
> http://www.snopes.com

In2books Clubhouse
> http://en.community.epals.com/book_club/default.aspx

Planet Book Talk
> http://www.smplanet.com/planetbookclub/novels

ePals™ Global Community
> http://www.epals.com

ePals™ Student Forum
> http://en.community.epals.com/student_forums1/f/default.aspx

Voices of Youth
> http://www.voicesofyouth.org

In2Books
> http://in2books.epals.com/login.aspx?ReturnUrl=%2fDefault.aspx

iEARN Collaboration Center
> http://www.iearn.org

The Teacher's Collaboration Projects
> http://www.theteacherscorner.net/collaboration-projects

United Nations Cyber School Bus
> http://www.un.org/Pubs/CyberSchoolBus

Chapter 8

iMovie®
> http://apple.com/apps/imovie

ShowMe
> http://showme.com

VoiceThread®
> http://voicethread.com

Lego 2
> http://www.youtube.com/watch?v=ITOaXPYaUCE

Death Is Calling
http://www.showme.com/sh/?h=JuJ13w0

MixedInk
http://www.mixedink.com

MixedInk Tool Overview
http://vimeo.com/10468404

Evernote®
http://evernote.com

Diigo®
http://diigo.com

Annotate®
http://branchfire.com/iannotate

DocAS
http://itunes.apple.com/us/app/docas-pdf-converter-annotate
/id437110885?mt=8

Chapter 9

TPACK Framework
http://www.tpack.org

International Reading Association
http://www.reading.org

Times Educational Supplement
http://www.tes.co.uk

Classroom 2.0
http://classroom2.0.com